ON CULTURE
AND COMMUNICATION

ON CULTURE
AND COMMUNICATION

The B.B.C. Reith Lectures 1971

By

RICHARD HOGGART

NEW YORK

OXFORD UNIVERSITY PRESS

1972

Library of Congress Catalog Number: 72-82674

PRINTED IN GREAT BRITAIN

For
Sammy and Billy
with love

Acknowledgements

I am very grateful indeed to the following people for help of many different kinds in the preparation of these lectures; Catharine Carver, Sally Cochrane, Lola Costa, Diamantino Do Vale, Philip French, Anne George, Josette Guidat, Stuart Hall, Douglas Johnson, Gretta Keenan, Denis Lawrence, Gail Lerner, Brigitte Le Varlet, G. E. T. Mayfield, Frank McDermott, Howard Newby, Lisbeth Schaudinn, Roy Shaw and, finally, my wife Mary.

CONTENTS

I

TAKING FOR GRANTED

I

Taking for Granted

I have called these talks *Only Connect*, taking the phrase from
E. M. Forster's novel *Howard's End*, because I am going to look
at the great variety of ways we have of getting in touch with each
other, and at the assumptions which lie behind those efforts to
get in touch about what our relations to each other should be.

My approach might seem odd to some people, so I ought to
say how I came to it. I have been making notes for years about
things which have struck me—incidents, remarks, gestures.
Just before we went to live in France for a while, almost two
years ago, I looked fairly casually through these notes and saw
that they were very often about private and individual ways of
making contact with others and especially about ways which
don't use words, about what the social psychologists call para-
linguistic or non-verbal communication.

I didn't at the time know when or how all this would sort
itself out; but France has been the catalyst. Living in a foreign
country you soon learn how much your ways of being in touch
depend upon belonging to a particular society, how much
they support both your society's sense of itself and your own
efforts to establish working relationships within it. So I will
begin by talking about being in touch in one's own society.
And I shall base what I say mainly on my own experience.
These are personal not specialist talks.

.   .   .

Most of the signals we pick up, especially when we are in our
own society, we pick up without knowing it. We are like
people who take part by ear in a very subtle, non-stop

symphony. This is true whatever education we have had and whatever our social class; and our idioms show it. Whenever you look closely at something very much a part of common experience, you find a range of subtle observations on it woven into everyday speech. Since I began thinking around this subject many old and apparently hackneyed phrases, phrases such as 'getting out of touch' and 'taking for granted', have come up mint-new. They point straight to the fact that so much in our communicating depends on the assumption of extraordinarily close relationships.

Take these, for example:

> You should have seen the look he gave me
> I gave her a meaning look
> Her looks spoke daggers
> She didn't say anything, but I knew what she was thinking

And here are two which have more than a single dimension. Each implies a set of relationships and a manner of speaking to match:

> Who do you think you're talking to?
> Don't use that tone of voice with me

It is easy to see that tone is more important than the dictionary-meanings of the words we use. Properly described, tone is a complicated matter of pitch, stress, timbre and the like. But I am using the word as a shorthand way of referring to those qualities in speech or writing which carry our sense of a relationship to another person. I want to get away from any remnant of the idea that tone is a dead carrier of live substance. Tone is part of substance; it can make the same words carry wholly opposed meanings. If you know your contexts it's simple to make 'Goodbye' mean: '. . . and I hope I never see you again' or '. . . and I can't wait to get back to you' or many points between.

Sometimes one can communicate effectively through the

spaces between words. I don't only mean deliberate silences for
effect. I mean pauses, unfinished bits, not used deliberately but
no less full of meaning. As in those conversations which never
quite touch a substantive or verb and which move, like fish
gliding past rocks and huge growths in those underwater films,
from 'you know ... sort of ... I mean ... like ... kind of'
all the way to the end, with gestures orchestrating the words all
the way too. And being understood. There is a corny old joke
about a West Riding working-man who had to be away from
home for a long time. His wife heard nothing from him. Then
one day he turned up, took his seat at the side of the fire, sat
awhile and finally said: 'Owt?' 'Nowt', his wife replied, and
that was the end of that conversation. I suppose it is meant to
show the droll taciturnity of Yorkshire people, but it just as
well shows that in some contexts most communication goes
on in the gaps between the words. Sometimes silence on the
part of one person is assumed, as an integral part of the act of
communicating. The hearer's place is defined by the speaker's
needs. It would be a mistake if he said a word; he has to listen
but in a certain way.

Words, tones, pauses make up very rich registers for speaking to each other. So do many other things, especially most
aspects of our appearance. Those too are ways of passing signals
to others. And to ourselves; they are means by which we support our own inner sense of ourselves, even in what may at
first glance seem very public situations. This is true both of
those parts of our appearance we can easily control, such as
dress, and those we have less day-to-day, conscious control over,
such as habitual gestures, expressions of the eyes, voice, face.

I am going to begin with some sketches towards social
readings or interpretations of manners and styles in England.
So these are home thoughts from abroad, especially about the
many signals you simply take for granted until you go away,
and about the ways we get in touch other than through words
—they are about eyes, voices, faces as ways of speaking.

Actually, eyes are used less, socially, than many other features. They *are* used in that way, it's true. There are such things as histrionic 'piercing' looks and—this one has become a cliché—the cocktail party quick flicker, when someone's eyes sweep the room on the lookout for more important people while they are supposed to be engaged with you. But more often eyes say something about the individual below the acquired social manners—from eyes assured of certain certainties to vulnerable, hurt eyes, or to eyes which go from you in a way different from that met in cocktail party situations. You may not be in a crowd at all; but the eyes facing you switch off as though an electric plug has been pulled, and they are no longer lighted outwards. You know that the person facing you is a long way off at that moment, living elsewhere and at a greater depth.

Voices are much more easily translated, socially, particularly in Britain. Most of us in Britain, perhaps because of their class qualities, seem almost as responsive to voices as to smells. One of the more marked English voices is that acquired by certain middle-aged, middle-class women. It is as much the sign of a group as what people used to call 'Billingsgate fishwife' to indicate one kind of harsh, working-class woman's voice. House-hunting in middle-class Birmingham, as we trailed from one desirable residence to another, we heard that middle-class voice again and again. Both the voice and the manner that goes with it are hard. They speak of a class defending itself and its one-eighth of an acre, as it has for centuries, against all those below: lazy workmen, fiddling shopkeepers, insolent public servants.

I once met an even more heavily-accented group, when by chance I spent a few days in an hotel with some barristers. They were quite amiable, though they found me at least as odd a bird as I found them. They enjoyed calling me 'Prof.', and the word rolled warmly off their tongues, slightly amused, even slightly impressed, slightly puzzled. Surely, their cultural stereotypes said to them, he should have a weighty presence. On my side, I was struck by the closed world they inhabited, and seemed to have inhabited since they were first sent to their prep. schools. Their closed or in-group speech made me feel out of it, in spite of their friendliness.

Most of them lived in exurbanite areas round London. They had all been to good public schools, and could read each other's signals immediately. They were all living within similar, invisible but unbroken plastic wrappers, moving easily towards old age inside them, within a society about whose other members they were not, and had not been inspired by their education to be, curious in an informed way. A certain anecdotal curiosity they could show, but that is easy. They were an assured group within a society about whose other groups, parts, history, they had sketchy but firm and most misleading views. Their ideas on 'the place of Britain in the world today', 'the working classes', 'the North', 'the student generation', were travesties; and they were confident within them. That part of the system into which they had been born had trained them to serve a view of the legal profession and its social relations which was not only inadequate but false.

If their legal procedures usually worked, in human terms— and they seemed to do so more than one would have predicted from their off-duty conversation—this was because, in spite of the reach-me-down social and psychological ideas they held, they could also draw on a tradition of reasonableness and undramatic honesty. They were sensibly buttressed in their practice not by abstract principles but by the fact that they didn't expect too much of men. They were not prigs; they knew chaps tended to get into scrapes. I remembered, years before, seeing a judge at the Old Bailey find it hard to follow the arguments, by both sides, about *Lady Chatterley's Lover*. But when disposing, in an interval, of some of the more usual and nasty kinds of case, he showed great wisdom and humanity.

B

Still, in the barristers I met, one couldn't help thinking that livelier imaginations would have been useful.

Most formal educations don't give much help in reading the signals of society closely or accurately. Think of English faces, for example. Years ago I became interested in faces, especially in the faces of middle-aged men. I remember the exact moment. A diesel coach pulled up at a small Lincolnshire village; I looked out and there on the almost deserted platform was Winston Churchill, dressed as a station master. Or a stationmaster pretending to be Winston Churchill? Not quite that, either; but a heavy man in advanced middle-age who had put up an expression like Churchill's.

How strange, and how difficult to interpret confidently. He had decisions to make in his job, and no doubt they could be worrying. Did they weigh as heavily on him as though he were the Prime Minister of a country at war? Or had he given way to a self-indulgent inflation of his role? Seen close-up for any length of time, would the heavily decisive Churchillian lines have turned out to be no more than a rough sketch? How much was his face for the world, and how much for himself?

But this begins to seem belittling and I don't intend that. One is tempted that way because the Churchillian face is, or was, so obvious a model for copying; it suggests kidding yourself. But other kinds of strength can be imprinted on faces, even though we assume that only the kind of faces which go with recognizably big jobs have a right to be taken seriously. I met not long ago, in a time of great personal crisis, a man with a job which, though responsible, would not in the usual ranking be thought important. He showed steadiness and a great ability to manage; he had, one soon saw, a very strong presence. What one learnt during that crisis, and what the usual social images would not necessarily have led one to expect, was that the presence was real. He had struck a balance which was effective and humane, struck it through facing and trying to resolve, day by day, difficult human problems in a setting which to the public eye would seem dull, unimportant, provincial in all the limiting senses. The public eye would have been wrong. Men of substance, if that phrase is to have any worthwhile meaning, are everywhere. It's a pity our range of recognized faces for strength, and for lots of other qualities, is so limited.

There are signals, especially of slightly insecure self-importance, at all levels. If you spend much time among professors you will be struck by the recurrence of a few styles. Most of them are not peacocky; folksy, perhaps, as a foil to the suggestion of learning worn lightly. I have seen the same professor move in a single two- or three-hour Faculty meeting from a pipe-ruminating, shrewd, academic statesman in his expression, his gestures and even his voice to a Northern no-flies-on-Charlie light-voiced urchin. Another professor puzzled me by an inverted comma effect around the radiance of his smile towards students. It was open, expansive, warmly assured. And yet, yet . . . something was being played that was not easy to hear. Then suddenly it clicked. It was the public smile of a handsome man, a man still handsome in middle age, who *knows* he is handsome.

If you stand on New Street Station, Birmingham, waiting for one of the fast morning trains to London, you find yourself in a crowd of middle-aged men mostly wearing elements of the same well-known uniform—the dark suit, homburg, good brief or executive case, rolled umbrella, pigskin gloves—and the same style of face; all in all a portliness, an air of substance, importance and seriousness. Solicitors, higher executives of Building Societies, officials of the big works and corporations, professors. Then, unexpectedly, you may have, without trying to be funny, a sharp, sudden vision of them all in their underwear in their bedrooms that night in Solihull or Sutton Coldfield, with their glasses off, talking to their wives, worrying about their daughters living in London bedsitters, each carrying on that attempt to make coherent, unified sense of his public and private life which for all of us finds its most common expression in a continuous conversation, sometimes in their presence, sometimes only in our own heads, with the person who is nearest to us, wife or husband; a process which is like the most elaborate, continuous knitting of a fabric that is always threatening to fall apart; but which we have to keep whole, and do usually manage to keep whole, because that is the basis on which our lives have whatever meaning they do have.

Then just as suddenly we come back to that railway station platform, near the point where the first-class carriages stop, on the morning of a full working day. How *do* we get, make, our faces? How to distinguish between what the society offers by way of a stock of translatable faces, what the inner personality of each of us forces on our face, and what the hazards of experience—illness, accidents, failure, success—engrain on it? It is the cheerful faces which puzzle most. One's instinct is to mistrust them, to assume they indicate some ingenuousness. But that could be to underrate the luck of good health, or be unjust to courage.

People, we assume, are much the same everywhere; personality will out, and the ups-and-downs of life are much the same everywhere too. Sure, but the ways these qualities and experiences express themselves differ in different societies. Each society has several ranges of typical face, and the distinctions between them become finer and finer as you look at them. There is a lean, quizzical, face one finds among clever men on the Eastern seaboard of the United States, the face of an intelligent man in a wide-open, mass-persuasive society who is not to be taken in, who has kept his cool and his irony. Such a face is not so likely to be found among its counterparts in Eastern Europe; the winds which beat on these men are different. Their faces are graver, more direct, and yet more reserved.

Because I have met them at some cross-roads in my own life, I am particularly interested in a range of faces which cluster round the idea of a public man in Britain. At his most characteristic, this man is in his middle-fifties. His appearance is what the whisky advertisements, giving it more of a gloss than it really has, call distinguished. His face is well-shaven but not scraped; it has a healthy bloom, but not an outdoor roughness; it is smooth, but not waxy. What is by now quite a full face is as solid as leather club-armchairs, and as decently groomed; it smells as good as the public rooms of those clubs. The hair is often marked by the appearance of Cabinet Minister's wings, that is, it is brushed straight back above the ears to plump out at the sides; it has a silvery sheen. The teeth are strong, one sees when the lips, as they readily do, curl back into a full, firm smile. They suggest someone who is used to talking in public and to deciding, to biting firmly into problems. They are wonderfully communicative teeth, and remarkable evidence that from all the possible ways of using teeth, the ways we smile or grimace, we select only some: we select from the codebook of tooth-signals in our society.

The coherence of the style is rarely breached. I remember one occasion which, because of its oddness, underlined how consistent that style usually is. One such public man—one who was apparently such a man—said to me, as we stood around in the intervals of a meeting: 'You see, Hoggart, I believe in the English people'. As he said it, it sounded naïve, a little self-important, touching, generous; but not sayable by a native English intellectual, least of all in that particular ambience. But he was a first generation European immigrant intellectual. His son is hardly likely to strike a false note like that.

Among the most striking in the line of public figures is the old–young man; and they are most often found in the higher reaches of education. These men are slim, with little trace of a paunch even at fifty-five; their faces still show the outlines formed when they were Head boys at their public schools or good day-schools. There is a French public type of about the same age who is in some ways similar; but the differences are interesting and, to me, unexpected. The French type is even leaner; he is also more elegant, better groomed, and more professional-looking than the Englishman. He is likely to have close-cropped hair and glasses with thin gold rims. It all fits with being called a 'haut fonctionnaire'. The English type is more casual, looser in the limb.

Englishmen of this kind are obviously energetic. They like to be irreverent, and are fond of cutting red tape. It is easy to be ironic about them and say: 'The steadiness of the half-shut eye'. But these men are not rigid. They get a lot done and their limits are not where one might assume. Even their occasional blokeishness is not really patronizing, unless you get further than usual into that word's meanings.

None of this gives a translation of personality unless you do a second and third reading. Granted that this is the pattern of available signals, and that their social meanings are thus and thus, what does that tell us about what any particular man wants to say to his society and to himself; what does it tell us about him at bottom? The justification for learning more about social vocabularies is that unless you understand what social signals you are responding to, all the time, you will be less likely to see through the groups of a certain age and style, and see the individuals within. But even that is not the right way of putting it; it is too anxious to see real character as the in-violate inner kernel of a fruit. In all of us our particular environments, our particular times and places, encourage certain sides and discourage others; and though these things may not be able totally to make character they have more effect than we usually admit. They filter and order the way we receive and respond to even our most powerful emotional experiences, those we would assume brought us face to face, nakedly, with our own character.

I have been underlining how complex are the day-to-day

social readings we all make. It follows that, even after years, we communicate relatively thinly in a society not our own. Some foreign signals are easy and can be read after a few weeks. The danger then is that we over-interpret them, lean on them too much so as to make up for the lack of density and resonance in our response. Not long ago I was lost before a new kind of face. Or, rather, I mistrusted my own reading of it; it was too easy and dismissive. This was a politician from the United States, a man who had been successful in oil or insurance well before he was forty and who now, in his middle forties, had an assured, thrusting, mercantile, tanned, smoothly smiling but tough look. To me the face, the whole manner, was two-dimensional, unmarked. It was like the face of a well-groomed dog. It said only: 'Public acquaintance ... manipulation ... action'; not: 'Friendliness ... thought ... feeling'. Had such a man, you wondered, ever felt shabby or insecure? Oddly, it was easier to imagine him crying. There was probably within the rhetorics available to him a form of crying that would do. But I was probably wrong, unable to read the signals in a way which got me near his character, which made him three-dimensional, capable of real grief and joy, unpublic. I couldn't easily imagine *him* in his underwear, and when I did he looked like an advertisement in ESQUIRE.

Inside our own society things may look easier; after all, we have the code-book for reading the signals which that society provides. But what we are given is an all-purpose, self-defining kit. We are given the styles and then the keys to them. They tend to be convenient keys, not always accurate keys; so we have to learn to break through the codes. It is easy to see the self-defining double process at work in the attitudes of those middle-class figures I talked about earlier. Our own attitudes may seem more independent, penetrating, and objective; but they are often just as much the product of a group's fashions, its ways of selecting and interpreting other parts of society. One of the main results of questioning yourself like this is being led step by step to see how many more clichés you have in your own baggage than you had thought. Not all of them have to be rejected. Sometimes you find they have, after all, to be kept; but by then they have been seen in new lights; you have a new hold on them so that they are no longer clichés.

One of the commonest sets of clichés are those which define the nature of suburban life. I'm struck now by the selectiveness of the picture they produce and by the extent to which they constrict the understanding of suburban life. That life can be even more grim than the clichés allow one to feel; it can also be more attractive.

It can be small-minded, keeping-itself-to-itself, fearful about status to a depressing extent. It can be claustrophobically turned in upon itself; as at moments during a grammar-school speech day when you can look around at all the carefully groomed mothers and fathers and feel the heavy weight of socio-academic anxiety bearing down on that platform. How can we be so totally engrossed in this particular bit of Western Hemisphere ritualism? How lacking in perspective can we get? You recall Auden's unpleasant line about 'The clerk going "oompah, oompah" to his minor grave'.

But Auden also wrote a poem called 'In Praise of Limestone' which can be seen as a tribute to aspects of suburban life, to the lives of people who are, in Auden's phrase: 'adjusted to the local needs of valleys'. In some ways, he is saying, people who settle for a domestic scale among others who have done the same, who have no great urge towards power or asceticism, may be in touch with important and neglected parts of our being. Their lives may not be full of striking contours; but they can now and again reveal some things about *not* going places, about one sort of harmony.

I once knew well a man and his wife who lived the most conventional of lives in the semi-detached suburbs of a Northern city. He was what is called a minor clerk and they had one very much loved daughter. All three were small—generations

of working-class city life in the North had brought that about.
He had, in his family's terms, done quite well for himself. Yes,
and they had a little car, too; the *lot*, according to the caricature.
The parents are dead now, and that particular home is gone as
though it had never existed. But to feel superior to all that, as
you walked along there on a bright Sunday morning, would
have been stupid. We all know the stock images . . . the whole
area smelling of roast beef, Radio 2 coming out of open
windows, the men at work in the garden or washing the car.
Still, there was above all a feeling of peace. When all has been
said about its limits, you have also to stand back and say how
much better this was, as a style of life, than many alternatives.
It was not aggressive; it was out to be neighbourly and it had
all sorts of well-practised ways of being so. On those Sunday
mornings, people really were living in the present, which is
what enjoying yourself means; they felt settled, comfortable
in their places, not looking for the next move. They did not
ask many questions about the good, the true and the beautiful;
nor did they tear one another apart. If we looked more closely
at suburban life we would see that it can at times achieve a
domesticity and neighbourliness which are a kind of quiet
triumph.

But that is only one possible example, chosen because
suburban life particularly attracts quick judgements from many
people. We can all be subtle interpreters of social signals. But
we like to limit the number of adjustments we make, whether
about suburban life or middle-class life or professional life or
academic life; or in interpreting faces, voices or gestures. And
our society, or more accurately the particular parts of society
to which each of us belongs, encourages us to limit our readings. All of which is a pity because if we looked more closely
we would—all of us, whatever our education—be surprised by
how much we had simply taken over unexamined. These talks
are about the strength of the readings offered by our cultures,
and about the need to reinterpret those readings for ourselves.

II

TALKING TO YOURSELF

II

Talking to Yourself

In spite of all I said in my first lecture about words being only one way of making contact, I am going to talk now mainly about getting in touch through words; or more accurately through tone, tone in writing. Getting in touch not only with other people but also, and first of all, with oneself. If we are writing about anything important to us we are both trying to speak to others and developing a relationship with ourselves. Finding a tone to talk with begins with finding one that seems right to and for us. Talking to others begins with talking to yourself and with being yourself in talking.

At this point we are set on a tricky journey, a potholing discovery of our own personalities through our characteristic ways of using words. We are discovering our mind's favourite movements in approaching events, in making manageable shapes out of experience. These movements are likely to be expressed by the repeated use of the same images, by the same kinds of stress at similar points, by certain favourite words. From all of these, one can quite soon make a rough cut-out of the shape of one's mind; and one will probably be surprised at its simplicity, at the way a few words are used like incantations or like flags to be saluted. Which shows that our thought is not pliant enough.

That kind of examination is relatively easy. We can go on and find worse. We can find ourselves using a range of stylistic tricks or tics in writing—insertions, conjunctions, pauses, exclamations, saving clauses, false loadings; they are all insurances, crutches, face-savers, hedgings of bets. Almost any of them can be used properly as signs that we are aware of other points of view, of qualifications. It is the over-use or the special

use at certain points which makes the difference. Here are some
common English examples:

> in one sense; in a way; perhaps; of course;
> it is precisely; we all know; naturally;
> I realize that; I suppose; in some respects

There are dozens of ways of trying—more often than not
unconsciously—to forestall criticism, to protect ourselves on all
fronts by means of stylistic devices, dozens of ways of cutting
corners, dozens of intellectual and emotional evasions. Our
nerve has failed and we are saying implicitly to the reader:
'Don't hit me and I won't hit you', or, 'You scratch my back
and I'll scratch yours'. By these favourite words, phrases and
movements we project desirable images of ourselves; but we
recognize them even less in our writing, I think, than in our
speech or our face-to-face styles and gestures.

It follows that, when we are in difficulties during writing of
this kind, we are likely to be avoiding ourselves as much as
others. When we start cutting corners we are avoiding the
risk, at that moment felt to be high, of stumbling on some truth
about ourselves. So it is we, ourselves, who get the biggest
shocks. We discover that some of the most telling—there's
another of these exact, everyday images; 'telling' means 'that
counts'—elements in our character were unknown to us;
though, we realize quickly, less unknown to others. Or at least,
though they were in a sense known to us, they were not faced
until, in the effort to write better, we came up against the
strength of their resistance. To discover one of these qualities
and face it, in my experience, is as difficult as to realize for the
first time that people talk about you in your absence, and as
strange and surprising as it is to discover just what they say
about you.

After a while connections, relationships one simply had not
known, begin to appear. I remember the first time I realized
how often I expressed righteous indignation in writing; and

then recognized that my ways of doing it were legacies from primitive Methodist chapel rhetoric. I remember, too, the moment when recurrent passages made me see that I felt especially easy with elderly women; and went on to see the connection between that and being brought up by my grandmother and spending a lot of time alone with her in the evenings. I remember, also, becoming suspicious of my own suspicion of authority in almost any form. That kind of movement in my mind, the change in the pressure of my writing at such points, was too obvious to ignore. It was easy, from some events in my life, to see how such an attitude towards authority could have developed; it presumably had the same origin as an over-quickness to react against being cut out. Being orphaned and receiving municipal charity could have helped it develop. But the feeling is so strong, and so much like a resentment, that I do not feel the explanations I have just given are adequate. I guess it will be difficult to trace this knot of resentment to its sources, and that if and when I do get there it may reveal some basic limitation in the cast of my mind; something not fully explained or justified by childhood experiences, something which takes away any grounds for regarding the attitude as laudable, a democratic stand against authoritarianism. It is, I already think, a disability, a blanking out of some responses, because it allows me to dismiss too easily a variety of attitudes in others. I am not at all suggesting that I ought to learn to respect authority. I am saying that the quickness, the lack of qualification and the pleasure in my rejecting authority, and the easily available rhetoric to express that rejection, seem to indicate an insensitivity, a dead area, in part of my mind.

Towards others there can be, in this kind of writing, a false candour by which one thinks of all possible weaknesses in oneself and puts them down frankly. It is a further deception. Perhaps people will assume we have risen above a fault when we have done no more than point at it. Perhaps we will even kid ourselves in that way. 'All censure of a man's self is oblique praise. It is in order to show how much he can spare', Dr. Johnson said. True, very often. But not always; and without taking the risks we may miss a lot.

In the end there are few successful ways of escaping. In writing of this sort you do not have the shield of form which the literary-social critic has, nor the shield of an academic discipline's formal approaches, nor the technical language which a social scientist has. Still, we are all of us, in the end, exposed in our language, whatever our particular field of work. 'Every man's work, whether it be literature or music or pictures or architecture or anything else, is always a portrait of himself' Samuel Butler said in *The Way of All Flesh*.

So the business is difficult. But yet, one can be sure, worth-while. When you are getting quite deep down, when your apparently irreparable inadequacies have begun to show and so your irremovable limits, when you are—in a sense you had not so much felt the force of before—face to face with yourself, that is at first depressing. But it is also—well, what word can one use? What word is possible in English that will not sound inflated? 'Liberating' is in some ways right but too grand to be usable. So you have to say simply that, when you have got used to the recurring shocks of self-discovery, the process seems worth going on with. At the least it is a relief: you do not have to pretend any more, even to yourself, about some things.

It is a double process. At the same time you are trying to learn more about your own personality, below the disguises offered by its defences; and you are also trying to find a style to express it. You feel a sort of isolation, a referring of every-thing back to yourself, which is not particularly pleasant. Yet I think we all have to go that way if we are to write better about personal experience. We have to go that way so as to find a style both for expressing ourselves and for being in touch with others.

It is difficult to know how far we can alter our styles by taking thought. To a great extent our styles are us and we had best make the best of them; in two senses—put up with them and bring out the best in them. To wish otherwise is like a small man trying to pretend he's tall. When I was young I used to wish I could acquire a full, flowing style—it was like the illusions one had singing opera in the bath. I wanted a long syntactical breath with lots of runs, contrasts, juxtapositions, ambiguities, interlacings, all with subtle variations of length and pace and tone and stress. I realized later that my style by nature doesn't have a long line, but moves by putting together short and idiomatic units—which may owe something to being brought up in a society which talked rather than read, talked in short periods, and used a lot of concrete metaphors. I wish I could carry better in writing the force of that tradition in speech. Few people have managed it, without being anecdotal or folksy; and that is quite different from creating a style which expresses the temper in facing experience that can be effectively carried in the spoken word.

Still, we do write for others as well as for ourselves. But who are the others we are trying to get in touch with? Turn around one of those old phrases I've quoted before, look at it from another angle, and ask again: 'Who do you think you're talking to anyway?' In all those 'We all ...' and those 'We know, of course' and those 'We should more often ...' what grounds are there for the sociable contract implied in the very use of the word 'we'? It's a cosy word, not by any means so easily accessible to, or necessarily admired by, writers in some other societies.

Who makes up the 'we'? Is it 'the intellectuals'? In Britain that doesn't sound right. It suggests a role for intellectuals, and relations with the intellectual life, which aren't true to the pattern of things here. Anyway, though it might in the abstract seem rather good to think of oneself as speaking to the intellectuals, that form of words suggests too much a closed group or clan.

Is one trying to speak to 'one's own generation'? A strange

phrase, that, and itself an intellectual's phrase, a standing-out-side and making-patterns phrase. The first time I heard it used by a member of my own generation it gave me a slight shock. It suggested a set of relationships and a placing in time which, though I found them neither off-putting nor particularly attractive, I simply had not thought of before; a sense of life as a going-along towards the end of our short period on the earth in a wide horizontal phalanx, within one's generation, chatting all the way. No doubt with odd looks forward and back, but generally moving forward within one's generation-band. A strange, interesting thought, though it does not greatly fit my own sense of who I think I'm writing to. Still, to some extent the idea of one's generation as the people who most ought to be reached, since with them one has especially shared experiences, must be involved.

Then there is the 'intelligent layman' and all the variants on that idea, here and abroad; the 'saving remnant', the 'common reader' (not the same, but none of the phrases is synonymous; cultural differences and historical changes prevent that); or the French *grand public cultivé*. You can play with *that* phrase for ages, and bring out some key differences between France and Britain. I would have liked to use the phrase 'the intelligent layman' because few of us can hope to be better than that outside our own specialist interests. But it seems unusable since it apparently suggests to some people a sort of patronage: that here is a writer looking out at the common people and hoping to do good to the few intelligent ones who will listen. Which is not what is meant at all. So I give up that phrase and the other approximations; they all send some people off on the wrong track. For all that, the idea that a writer can and sometimes should write for a wider group than his close fellows, an idea which is miles away from what is suggested by a word like 'popularization', this idea has been active in British writing for at least two hundred years and tells a great deal about one main quality in British social life.

It suggests that there are people, whom one can think of as a kind of group, who are interested in questions outside their specialism or may not have a specialism at all, people who are interested in ideas outside their professional ambitions, people who read or listen because they simply assume it matters to do so. Some such people are bound to be intellectuals, obviously; and they include professional people. But it is a disposition of mind we are talking about, not a matter of training or family background. So people in this group may not be intellectuals in the usual sense (in other ways they may be true intellectuals). During the Second World War Arthur Koestler wrote about what he called 'the anxious corporals', who carried Pelicans in their battledress and sought each other out. It's a pity but not surprising that by that point in the twentieth century it took an immigrant intellectual to recognize that such people existed. By today, the pressures to compartmentalize training and taste have almost erased the memory.

I was an adult education teacher for twelve years and the basis of that kind of teaching is, first, the coming together of mixed groups of people of the sort I have described; and, second, the idea (which can be made quite free from cant) that a good class is a joint enterprise in which the tutor is learning no less than the students. But the implications of this whole range of attitudes go far wider than education. They contain the unspoken assumption that a society is or should be a community, have a kind of unity; a sense which crosses classes and other divisions, and crosses particularly the divisions implied in the very use of such phrases as 'the intellectuals', let alone 'the masses'? What is the origin of this sense that a society ought to be able to talk within itself *as a whole*, should not all the time and need not all the time be divided; and of the feeling that, in spite of all the great and maybe increasing obstacles, it is still just possible in Britain to talk like that?

It is, as I've said, a notion very deeply embedded in British culture. For all their differences, the manners used by many of those social critics who have written about the impact of industrialism for nearly two centuries—say, from Coleridge to Orwell—have much in common. They are talkative, as one individual to another, personal, direct, particular. And yet, one comes back to the question again: does it really survive, this sort of audience; or is it an out-of-date idea hung on to by a very few intellectuals, their equivalent of that myth of Britain's present international importance held by the barristers I mentioned in my first lecture? Certainly the idea gets a lot more lip-service than genuine service. It involves not only the assumption that one should try to talk to and listen to people outside one's specialism; for writers it implies also that—provided specialist technicalities are removed—many readers can take as much as most of us can offer; it involves therefore recognizing that to write in this way (if you call it either 'popularization'. or 'haute vulgarization' you are implicitly patronizing) is not a matter of writing-down, taking our complex truths, adding water and serving up with a few pally gestures. It is much more a matter of recognizing the extent to which many of our professional languages are unnecessary and defensive; recognizing that we have first to work hard so that, if we are lucky, we may write in a way which is equal to the new demands.

Full-time academics, with a few remarkable exceptions, were never much interested in this kind of writing, and still today most academics who do agree to speak to people outside their professionalism do so with little thought about what is involved; they often vulgarize the substance of what they have to say so that one detects an underlying—well, 'contempt' would be too harsh a word, but 'belittling' is not. One can hardly expect them to recognize, therefore, that some of the people who most try to grapple with these problems nowadays—and in very hard situations, under the pressure to compete for mass audiences—are professional broadcasters, men who want ideas to be made as widely available as possible without unnecessary obscurity or dilution, and who realize that what may seem an amorphous mass is always less than its individual parts.

But it is important to come back to the idea of a society talking within itself, as a whole, since that idea cannot simply be taken for granted. From time to time one meets someone who rejects it completely, who seems convinced in his bones that such an assumption is a delusion; that a society doesn't work that way, and can't; and that he wouldn't want it to. He believes those are not the terms of life but that we are all really alone. It is an unwarmed attitude, not very pleasant, often sardonic—but maybe right, after all. Certainly not everyone wants to be in touch, outside a small carefully chosen group; and some of those who don't are the most intelligent amongst us.

So it is one thing to feel there is a possible audience, but quite another to be in touch with it in that way, which starts by your trying to be honest to yourself, that I described earlier. Not that there is a shortage of *apparently* usable tones for writing in English. There are a great many tones. All of them, unless they are remade for our own person and voice, are barriers. Barriers between us and our material; barriers between us and the people who read us; barriers between us and those parts of our personality we need to reach down to. They are smooth, they are easily picked up, they can give a range of pleasantly-acceptable images of ourselves. And they are all useless if not fought for. They all implicitly assert staggeringly assured but unproved relationships. So that sometimes, after stumbling along trying to find your own style and falling again and again into those of others, like a tired walker hampered by falling into other men's tracks, you find yourself wishing for a totally neutral style, a style which assumes no relationships at all, with anyone outside.

As so often, there is a paradox here. Many tones in English are intimate in one sense. Most of the tones within which literary criticism is conducted, though not strictly personal, are enclosed and known, full of unexamined ideas about intellectual modes and contacts. The result is that that close-up intimacy itself, because it has been too easily assumed, distances. It becomes an invisible but impenetrable film; it separates both the writer and the reader from the shock of the experience being written about. Most easily reachable tones, no matter how sophisticated they may seem, neuter or reduce experience by distancing it and framing it. They cut it down, thin it out so that it fits the assumptions carried within the tone about the limits of the permissible, emotionally.

'The limits of the permissible, emotionally'—there is a whole new element there: the emotional inhibitions of British writing today. Learning to write with that more direct relationship to experience I described at the start means that we must at times be personal, and at times personal about matters which are strongly emotional. This is difficult in itself. And the lack of suitable tones to express emotion or, rather, the excess of tones which seem designed to mute emotion makes things harder. Even worse: because we are so used to denying or tailoring emotion it is difficult to know when our emotions are genuine. That must be got through, because the main point of trying to offer, as directly as we can, some experiences from our own emotional life is so as to imply not: 'Aren't I interesting and sensitive' but: 'This particular experience seems to have a more than personal meaning'.

To this, one of the most important aspects of this kind of writing, reactions can be sharp. Some people resist any attempt to draw from them even a small measure of shared feeling, as though that would knock them off a perch they have made to view the world from an emotional distance. For people like that, one of the worst weaknesses is to let your emotional shirt flaps show.

Criticism like this helps, far more than praise, to define the limits and the disciplines in this sort of writing. So do the more qualified reactions of those people, less driven by a personal edge, who are nevertheless wary of discursive trading in the emotions because they feel it is usually safer to meet on more testable ground. They remind those of us who are literary that we have a tendency to overcharge our material, to turn every face-to-face anecdote into a highlighted novelistic cameo, and in our writing to sell short the effort needed to make personal experience exchangeable, to think we can bring out its representativeness by a rhetorical sleight of hand, smuggling it in on its interestingness. All this, they suspect, distorts. They think that if we come to writing in that state of mind we will produce confidential rhetoric and deserve to be mistrusted.

This is very useful; but it does not prove that the main effort is not worthwhile, the effort to write and read with a more direct relationship to emotional experience. The relations between thought and feeling are not well made in Britain today, and not only in British writing. That so many styles and tones are ways of shielding us from the impact of making those links has, no doubt, a long and complicated history. But it is time we altered, in all sorts of ways, and looking at our manner of writing is one. This gap affects all parts of society. It can be seen most obviously in many of the decisions made by public authorities about social issues, about housing, medicine, education, the environment generally. Below these obvious examples of emotional undernourishment lie more difficult questions about the effects of that lack on our private lives.

But why should one assume that one's personal experience can ever have more than a personal meaning? That conviction is sometimes strong; yet what proof can there be of the validity, significance, truth, representativeness of the experience?

None, I think, in the end. We look at our own lives, we find ourselves returning to some occasions in them because they seem to be what Virginia Woolf called 'moments', to have a symbolic force, to be telling incidents. We feel also that they probably tell something about other people's lives, in this kind of society, here and now. And so we begin to move, gingerly, to make contact across the gaps.

There is no final assurance. We may feel in our bones that a moment is true, representative and all the rest. And we may write about it as exactly as we can. At the end we may have one of those rare moments of satisfaction when we feel quite sure it is true, etc., etc. Five minutes later we are wondering whether that experience wasn't just as subjective as any other, and quite *non*-significant, was selected and highlighted under the pressure of some parts of our personality which give it no particular representativeness or larger significance. It may have felt different from other experiences; it may have seemed to command assent beyond the needs of our own personality. But perhaps it was after all only a more complex echo from our own cultural armoury or our own basic mental patterns.

I have been talking about getting straighter with oneself in writing, the better to talk to others. Yet are we thinking of others when we are actually writing, when we are drawing on personal experience and trying to make sense of it? And if we do think we are writing for others, why are we doing so? To persuade them? To be admired? I expect most of us would give a carefully qualified yes to both those questions. But if we take one more step, and ask ourselves whether we want to persuade our readers to our point of view, or want their admiration, *at the expense of* what we think is the truth of what we are saying, then I think most of us would answer no.

So finally we are not, in any of the obvious senses, writing for others. We hope they will listen, but we are prepared to lose them in the last resort. We try not to trim; though maybe unconsciously, below the levels we can at present reach, we do trim.

If this way of looking at the matter is correct, then we write first for ourselves, for a more secure sense of ourselves, so as to hold steady a bit more of life, so as to feel less swayed-all-ways by the flow of experience. It is here that 'the others' come in, this time with more importance. Most of us would hate finally to feel alone. So one purpose of writing is to feel more securely, beyond simple assertions or crying down the wind, that we are not alone. We hope that this sort of effort will help us to reach more convincing ways of speaking to each other. It is therefore true in the end to say that part of the purpose of writing is to reach others; not to sell them anything or persuade them, but quite simply to be in touch. It follows that we best speak to others when we forget them and concentrate on trying to be straight towards our own experience, in the hope that honestly-seen experience becomes exchangeable. At this point the two themes—speaking to yourself and speaking to others—come together. They are not two directions; they are one and inextricable.

III

IN ANOTHER COUNTRY

III

In Another Country

Living abroad makes you think as you have not done before about the relations between the different parts of a society, about what each part assumes about those relations, and how that affects the way the different parts speak to each other.

At the start, you have a strong feeling of distance from *any* society. You are so out of touch that you feel impalpable. You can't 'take much for granted', to an extent that gives that old expression a yet sharper meaning; you are nearly tone deaf. I have been living in France for two years now and am just beginning to feel able to make rough comparisons. Much, even most, in French behaviour I still can't read. If you think of French society as a highly-developed living organism, then I am beginning to trace one or two striking constituents of its nervous system, and those chiefly because they differ so much from some British characteristics.

That must all sound agoraphobic. You don't feel homesick; that's not the right word. You feel starved and lost; in a large featureless landscape unable to read any of its signs, with your cultural suckers wavering anxiously to find something that they can clamp on to and draw nourishment from. You realize again how closed and known your particular sub-culture is. In my case it is that area where academics and writers and intellectual journalists signal to each other; and you realize how domestic and small-scale British society as a whole can seem.

This sense of the small, known, enclosed quality of most kinds of life in Britain first struck us fifteen years ago, on a year's visit to the United States. We carried over the usual stock of attitudes to America, and we found that they were almost all wrong. They were not truths about America; but they showed truths about the British, selecting and distorting American evidence to fit their book. In such a situation you are less prepared than if you had come with no views at all.

For us as for so many Europeans the American scene at first sight seemed to have little depth, little perspective or weight of back-cloth. So many American towns, no matter how long established or large and technological, seemed like clearings; temporary, likely to be discarded by a people constantly on the move; even though those people could show a pride in their towns of a kind which is rare in Britain. The long, low, open-plan houses with their front gardens open to the road, all that sense of horizontality and diffusion, were slightly unnerving. You wanted markers, hedges, fences, doors that could be shut, stairs which defined the areas of a house.

Conversely, things on the move, especially the large, garish cars, looked more right than they do in Britain, right for the endless straight roads and the bright light. That large-boned, rangy looseness you met in many of the men made you feel agoraphobic too. I kept remembering a typical figure from the town landscapes of Yorkshire before the Second World War—a little man, slightly bow-legged, in a flat cap and a dark boiler-suit, waddling quickly up a narrow snicket on his way home after the shift.

In such situations your puritanism is always coming to the front, tempting you to a sour rejection, to an old sweat's 'hold fast is your only dog', bloody-minded dismissal. The first sight of a large supermarket, at a time when Britain was still short, produced in me an extraordinary mixture of greed, scorn and fear. There'd be a dreadful reckoning for all this overabundance, sure enough. 'You'll pay for this'! You always do have to pay for your excesses. But that was to read American signals from a British code-book.

Or take the so-called American passion for goods, which makes us call them consumer-mad and invoke 'Americanization' as a swear-word whenever Europe takes yet another step on the road to the consumer society. Americans do love objects, products, new things that work or make things work. But if you live in an American community what you chiefly notice, after the shock of seeing so much stuff lying around, is precisely that it does lie round, isn't locked up or treasured in the European sense, but is easily lent or given away. We might produce another sour British phrase to explain that: 'easy come, easy go'. But we'd be wrong. The American love of goods is a transcendental love; it is not greedy or amassing. They love goods for what they say, romantically, about America, about rich resources and energy and the ability to make things work. That, and giving them away, is all part of the view they like to have of themselves. Large gestures are in line with the sense of possibility, of continuous expectancy; or it did still seem so back in the late 'fifties. This may seem an ingenuous attitude but it is not mean or calculating. And even the advertisements, much larger and bolder than in Britain, strike you—especially after a visit to Eastern Europe—as more than just bearable; they look like a tribute to the notion that there are areas of quixotic, wilful, free play; where *you* are free to swerve and dive and save yourself from being hooked, and *he* is free to tempt you with multi-coloured baubles. This, though it shouldn't be overemphasized against the gross pressure of persuasion in commercial democracies, is still part of the air of these societies. It is trivial and it tells lies about the terms of life. But they are lies many of us want to hear, and we are at least free, marginally, to make up our own minds whether to listen or not. The visual appearance of the society is not imposed from outside in terms of someone else's single, set view of the way things should be.

A remark by an Englishman I quoted in my first lecture—'I

believe in the English people'—was, I said then, hardly likely
to be made by a native English intellectual. But I remember a
third generation American, a professor with a good critical
mind, saying, when we were talking about the difficulties of
intellectual life in America: 'Still, you see, I'm proud of being
American'. I don't know whether he would actually say it
today, though at bottom he might still believe it. It didn't
sound embarrassing, there on an American sidewalk. Such a
man's sense of his relation to his country is, not necessarily
better or worse, but certainly different from that of an English
intellectual. The American remark reminds you that America
was willed as a social contract (or has told itself that that is
what happened) which was an assertion about the possibility of
creating a workable community by will. 'We willed this
system; let's make it work' lies at the back of much American
rhetoric, even when it has turned sour on itself. There is
a remark in Emerson, I think it is, about the importance
of the optative mood in America, the sense of possibility;
and I always remember, if I am tempted to make jokes
about her as she walks in a group the streets of Paris, Henry
James's touching remark about the American girl having a
permanent exclamation mark between her eyebrows. That's
expectancy.

Against this, one of the standard English moods is unexpectancy. 'He never expected much'; here, as so often, Thomas
Hardy touched a main strand in British attitudes. The small
land, the unexpansive climate, the whole lived-into social
structure, especially as it has borne on the great body of
working people, all conspire to lower the imaginative sights.
We are an unexpectant society and our unexpectancy can
make us illiberal, the inhabitants of worlds only penetrated,
if at all, down narrow, dark, brown, halls lit by 25-watt
bulbs.

That unexpectancy can also be a strength, as we often tell

ourselves. It can give a doggedness, a slowness in being over-borne by trouble, and a refusal to strike histrionics. You expect little, and you expect to soldier on. By contrast much in American friendliness and expectancy seems more self-conscious, less in the bone, less resistant to pressure. So that when it breaks down, as it has in some of the big cities now, the nakedness is instantly apparent, and appalling.

Still, people aren't so easily bracketed. A thirty'ish American wife with two children, destined to be on the move every few years because her husband was going up a salesman's ladder, once made to me almost with a wail a remark which captured the poignancy of one kind of mobile American. She couldn't settle in Rochester, four or five hundred miles upstate from their former home in New York, she said; and then, after a pause: 'Even the disc jockeys are strangers'. It caught so much about the lack of a lived-into community and about the role of the mass-media-created pseudo-communities, that it seemed like a title for an essay with the sub-title: 'On rootlessness and the role of the mass media'. But you didn't feel superior for long. She put out her roots very quickly indeed. I say 'out' rather than 'down' because she had no time to strike vertically like a plant; but she had learned ways of running out roots horizontally to pick up friends and neighbours; tough and twiny roots, not brittle. It would have been wrong to use a word like 'shallow'. Once she had begun to be physically settled and found time to turn round, she made a home, under the pressures of newness and of her husband's nervousness before the strains of his new job, which drew on her Italian ancestry far more than on persuasion by disc-jockeys or advertisements. It was good to sit in her kitchen, eating home-made hambone and pea soup, whilst she chattered away in her extraordinary drawl. *There*, her roots were feet thick and had never been cut.

Of the countries I know it is from France that one gets the sharpest sense of the nature of one's own society. Again the clichés fail and have to be thrown away or remade. Take the different attitudes towards the intellectual life in France and in Britain, the different assumptions about the place of intellectuals. France, I was taught, is an intellectual society, a society in which the intellect is respected and intellectual life flourishes.

Certainly, the sense of a public role which a French intellectual can still have, not just as a *cher maître* with his circle but as an actor out in the streets defying the *forces de l'ordre* by a flagrant, well-publicized and perhaps violent breach of the law, together with students and workers from the car factories, because they all feel that the pressures of authority are onerous —all this differs sharply from Britain. French intellectuals believe that the intellectual life is meshed in with the public life, that the life of the mind and especially of social analysis matters publicly, and that therefore they have *as intellectuals*, as a distinct social group, a valid public field of action; English intellectual life in comparison seems to lack conviction that it is seriously connected to public issues at all.

Or one thinks of French public debate at its best, its directness, clarity and unsentimentality. To hear one of the more intelligent French civil servants or politicians take part in argument is to be impressed by the achievement of a highly-centralized civilization and by the power and effectiveness, in their own terms, of the Grandes Ecoles. Then you remember that most British debates, in either House, about any issue on which some solid intellectual background is needed show a lack of the practice of thought, or even a lack of respect for the disciplines of thought. The British do deliberately play down intellectual eloquence as not reliable, not practically effective; and there is some sense in that. But we could do with some of the discipline of French argument.

In what ways, though, can French intellectuals be said to be in touch with their society? What are their relationships with its various parts, other than with the intellectual group or the intellectual tradition? What relations do they have, other than a fighting relationship with power and authority, a contempt for the bourgeoisie, and a political or intermittently romantic relation with the working-class?

I happen to have been connected with a similar issue in both Britain and France. This was the problem posed in the last two decades by the pressure from massive new numbers for entry to higher education. In France, the universities had swollen enormously but provision had not kept pace. Nor, good exceptions always readily admitted, had much changed in the attitudes of the staff. It had been clear to some people for some time that something would have to give, probably violently.

It gave in May 1968. The French had another revolution and afterwards, as is the practice, there had to be a major reform. So the *loi d'orientation*, the new deal in higher education, appeared. It is in many respects a brilliant, imaginative and attractive law. It wasn't thought up overnight; it could draw on a lot of thinking from well before the events of May. Still, it was made law almost overnight. It was a *tour de force* by the new minister, Edgar Faure, who drafted it and put it through with a speed which would have turned British Parliamentary draftsmen grey.

It can still, more than three years later, hardly be called fully working. Some people, not to be shaken by mobs in the streets or what they regard as a flashy law, have from the start been out to circumvent it in any ways they can, and their efforts have been made easier because its provisions can be interpreted so as to fit the letter but not the spirit. Some students mistrust it and they are out to wreck it too. Others, students and staff, are putting enormous efforts into trying to make the new law work in the right ways.

It seems to me that speed and intellectual elegance were bought by not sufficiently acknowledging the braking-force of some elements in French culture. Not only the slowness we can all show in appreciating the difference between a good democratic assertion and the enormous cost in public money of honouring it; not only the French academic's quite special inventiveness at digging-in against pressures to change his habits; but in particular some thick tentacular roots running through French society and especially through the bourgeoisie, roots which in this case bind people to such ideas as that of open access to the universities if you have the *baccalauréat*, or that of a degree centrally validated for the whole of France. The *loi d'orientation*, for all its brilliance, ran against the grain of some powerful attitudes towards education and its relation to social class and family in French life. It was not mediated in ways and by stages to make it square with those attitudes. It was as though one part of society wasn't listening to the other, and assumed that what it had created with such intellectual verve was so self-justifying and self-evident that the very creating and willing should bring it to pass.

The contrast with the British way of going-on is remarkable, and not necessarily to the credit of the British; I'm not making that sort of comparison. Faced with a similar movement, Britain, like a mole in the earth, went through a long process of adapting and adjusting, and finally produced a reasonably humane but quite unradical set of accommodations. It was a sort of slow surge over the years, for anyone in the thick of it, like—the mild animal images seem unavoidable—being on the back of a cow as it slowly turned over. There were endless discussions for and against expansion in the Press, in journals, on radio and TV; there were government committees and commissions of varying sizes and effectiveness; there were speeches and debates in both Houses (not very intellectual but concerned to get something done) and at a great variety of annual conferences; there were small groups privately at work; there was a mixed group of front-runners: two or three educational sociologists, a few headmasters, one or two vice-chancellors. They kept the debate moving and linked to practice in all kinds of ways known to such people, who run a shuttle service between Whitehall, the universities, the Press, the BBC, the main voluntary bodies. The whole operation was brought about by several different *kinds* of people, but there were relatively few of them as compared with the numbers actually affected by the changes. It would be pleasant to say that discussion in all the Senior Common Rooms of the country probed into the relationship between maintaining the best in university provision and accommodating many more students; that it looked closely, for instance, at the implications for methods of teaching. Readjustments *were* made and, for a number of mixed reasons, expansion was accepted. But common room discussion was often of a nagging, backs-to-the-wall kind. Few people felt that what they said would have much effect on what was decided. Most academic staff drifted into expansion.

In short, here was a classic cameo of how opinion gets formed and changed in Great Britain; this is the nearest the British usually get to what one might call a continuous, public debate.

As a result more money was increasingly made available for expansion, by governments of both parties; not as much as some of us hoped but far more than would have seemed likely a decade or so before: not enough to provide places in universities, properly so called, to meet all the demand; but other parts of higher education expanded too. The expansion in the universities themselves was achieved in ways which did not spoil their essential character, though that is a judgement not everyone shares. It did not result in enormous and anonymous classes. The proportion of staff to students, which is very high indeed by most international comparisons, was kept high enough to maintain that weekly small group teaching which British universities rightly think important.

The British manner of going about things showed a society which, though not particularly intellectual, had a sense of itself as a sort of whole and had lines of communication open between several different groups: politicians, civil servants, academics, intellectuals, intelligent laymen, journalists. So the decisions which were eventually made at each stage did not too much affront deep-seated attitudes in the culture, or its capacity to digest change at any particular moment; they were not so far out of line or so far ahead as to invite being rejected, ignored, bypassed. They ran, in their reasonable accommodations as much as in their limitations and cautiousnesses, along the grain of the society. They had been arrived at by an almost biological-seeming process of change over several years, itself an indication of similar changes of attitudes in many people in different parts of the society. You could not say the changes were inspired, led or dominated by the centre, whatever that is. When they came, the changes were not dramatic and they compromised. They were not based on a radical look at social and educational relationships. Some very powerful restrictions on the terms of the debate were all the time at work underneath, and they muted change. There was a general, unstated agreement not to go too far, there was much submerged paternalism, concerned to make the best available, as far as 'seemed reasonable', to the healthy adolescents who were the first post-war generation; and there was some hidden snobbery; the universities attracted attention more warmly and more easily than the secondary modern schools or other parts of higher education. But on the whole the new approach was decent and well-meaning, not predominantly meritocratic or out to make cheap imitations of Oxbridge. It eventually carried most people with it. The stresses of change were never so great nor the resistances to change so rigid as to cause a breakdown.

I said earlier that to be part of this change was like being on the back of a cow as it slowly turned over. She has finished turning over for the time being. By now the British seem to feel—'feel' is a better word than 'think' to describe these turning-points—they have absorbed about as much as they can for a while of the movement towards democratization in higher education; and the universities have virtually stopped growing. Some people within the universities can now ease themselves back into their chairs and try to carry on as if nothing had happened, nothing that challenged their views on higher education and on the spread of ability. All of which is sad because, since the fundamental issues were not faced, and they go far wider than the question of university expansion alone, the main problems are still with us.

In France the debate about higher education and its relation to French culture as a whole goes on energetically and has learned a great deal from '68. On this subject, France is now less enclosed, readier to listen to, and try to learn from, other countries' experiences, even to recognize that the British way of going about things can have something useful to show about established habits and their relation to change. After all, the proportion of working-class children in British universities is far higher than in French universities; pragmatism has worked better in that respect, over the years.

What I've been saying so far is connected with yet another commonly-held view about French society: that it is deeply divided. I suspected that idea at the start; I had heard it played with too often. Now I think it is true, because I can only make sense of French differences in manner, even within the same people at different times or in different settings, by having in mind the idea of opposed worlds. On the one hand are those outside, who are not us, who may be against us and whom we are at the least cautious towards: the government, the authorities, the powers-that-be, the Protestants, the Catholics, the Parisians, the provincials, the intellectuals, the bourgeoisie, the workers. There is an 'Us' and 'Them' feeling in Britain, too, but of a less marked kind. In France you don't expect to feel particularly tolerant to people outside your known circles. Nor do you expect, at any rate in Paris, particularly gentle public relationships. I suppose this may be related somewhere to the acceptance of violence as a part of the process of political life, though I'm not yet sure of that. What I do notice in Paris is a quickness to anger, and a level of contemptuous bloody-mindedness, especially in some public functionaries, that is thinner-skinned than the bloody-mindedness you so easily find in Britain. Britain has a highly-developed tradition of low, resentful, public rudeness, especially in minor public servants. But I have not seen in London people pushed or butted off the pavement by middle-aged, apparently middle-class men or women.

French driving illustrates some of these characteristics with an exactness which makes you suspicious, but which stands up on a closer look. It is a matter of high speeds and small margins; it is, by any reasonable safety standards, violent, self-regarding and dangerous. It is also accomplished and precise; it has a panache and sparkle which makes British driving seem sedate and dull. That's why so many Parisian cars carry their scars on them, unrepaired, like tomcats given to brawling.

This kind of quality in French life, once you learn to cope with it, can have a tonic effect. What it is saying about the public relationships it assumes is certainly not said evasively or larded over. It is not saying we are members one of another. There is a sense in which Frenchmen are deeply committed to the idea of France, the uniqueness of being French, and this might seem to bring them all together. In that way, at one level, it undoubtedly does. Yet you can love 'la France' but not other Frenchmen. The French love the family, but they are not so likely to describe France herself as a family in the way writers can still, no matter how drily, still sometimes apply the word to Britain.

'Us' and 'them'. In France, 'us' means above all the family.

The sense of the family is reinforced by and it reinforces the sense of others outside who are *not* family. The family is a close unit which demonstrates enormous powers of self-defence. Once you are in the family, even as a temporary member, the atmosphere changes. Now you are one of us; far from being cold towards you we will help you generously, as a matter of course, and we will stand with you against others, those outside. Associate membership can be extended to almost anyone you have got to know *as a person*, perhaps because you meet them regularly in some helpful context or, more important, because some human act has passed between you: a joke, a small kindness. The suddenness with which the guard drops and the friendliness with which you are then received throws into even greater relief the wariness assumed in public relationships. Once you have been accepted in this way you feel a warmth not at all as well provided for in the range of common attitudes for acquaintanceship we have in Britain.

For all that, French society is still markedly divided by classes; or, to put it more narrowly, in Paris one has a sense which one doesn't any longer have in London of the still dominant presence of the bourgeoisie; of the massive presence of the Paris workers too, when they break out. But, after all, they are then breaking out against a feeling of an habitual dominance by others. So many of the huge bourgeois apartment buildings are still fully in action, still occupied by and run for 'Them'. You may look out over the city and see the mansarded roofs of those eight and nine-storey blocks, and know that a great many of the attic rooms, *the chambres de bonne*, are still occupied by servants. Not nowadays by French country girls, but by Spaniards, Portuguese, and other immigrants, often living a village life up there, husbands and kids and all, in several generations. The French Revolution was a bourgeois revolution; it has had no effective successor.

A sense of the importance of hierarchy and of the deference due at the top is still strong. The hierarchical tones of voice persist; they tend to be high-pitched and urgent. The assumption of class-based power and hierarchy includes also a range of attitudes to the arts and intellectual life different from those of the dissident French intellectuals I described earlier. I mean the sanctified high bourgeois culture; that culture which the 'non-public' ignores (there's a revealing phrase, invented by a Frenchman to describe those who don't or can't or won't make use of the usual high cultural provision in the arts). That culture does have a respect for the arts and the mind. But it seems increasingly out-of-touch today because it expresses itself so much in fixed social terms, styles, tones.

If you watch French television through peak time on Sunday evening, on the one colour channel, you are likely to be struck by the high-bourgeois assumptions behind much of the programme planning. The stress on the high arts, on Quai d'Orsay or Grande Ecole assumptions about what is important, is remarkable. A discussion programme follows an arts programme and is followed by a long interview with a famous man. They are many of them fine programmes for well-educated and cultivated people. It is the missed chances one regrets, the rareness with which television seems to have been regarded as an opportunity to develop a new medium so as to reach new audiences for new kinds of good programme, not for the transmission of received forms, from other media, designed to cater for restricted groups, at other times.

I am not arguing for a populist lowbrowism, and I am not saying television should simply go for mass audiences at peak times. I am saying that television poses strongly the question of a society's sense of itself and of the nature of the possible audiences outside. Television should be experimental, but not in an aesthetic or technical way only. It should be constantly testing its own potentialities. Those are best found from the interaction between the possibilities of the medium and the texture of the society; that society will always be in a state of change and always more varied than most of us want to realize.

IV

THERE'S NO HOME

There's no Home

If you work in an international organization staffed by people of many nationalities you become much more sharply aware of the power of known cultural habits, the power of that invisible fabric which helps national societies to hold together. I am at present working at the Paris Headquarters of UNESCO, the United Nations Educational, Scientific and Cultural Organization, and in this lecture will be drawing on my experience there. Such organizations are non-cultures. Of course, they have qualities which allow them to be called subcultures in the sociologist's sense; but to start on that trail too soon is to miss the chance to make useful distinctions. Sometimes you wish you could rescue the phrase 'rootless cosmopolitanism' from being a term of abuse; used neutrally it would quite well describe the sort of society we live in, professionally. There are both gains and losses. Even more than when you are living in a national culture not your own, there is hardly anything you can take for granted, and you very often feel compass-less. You learn a lot about disorientation, new kinds of fear, and especially about your own weaknesses under unaccustomed stresses, in environments without signposts; you also learn a lot about the weaknesses and strengths in other men, whatever their nationalities or backgrounds.

It will be best to start with the difficulties of language, written and spoken, the addiction of international organizations to what Edmund Wilson called: 'this pompous, polysyllabic and relentlessly abstract style'. All the epithets apply; and though I am going to try to explain why some of them arise, the majority are unjustifiable. But in all large organizations there are verbal fashions, especially in those with intellectual or artistic features. 'Viable' was very popular in the BBC a few years ago: 'I think that should make a viable programme', they used to say. The current vogue for the 'in' and 'inter' words in what are called, oddly enough in itself, 'the members of the United Nations family'—for 'infrastructure', 'input', 'interface', 'interpersonal', 'interdisciplinary', 'intersectoral' and the others—is not a meaningless collective tic, though it is monotonously repetitive and often a substitute for thought.

The United Nations agencies will no doubt go on producing other comic examples of their unresonant jargon. It is likely to appear wherever many people are using a language not their own, for thoughts not their own, but for the 'higher executive' expression of the intentions of a large group of very differing governments, exceptionally trying to reach a common intellectual accord. Sometimes it tolls like a knell

> The exercise was observed with approbation because it afforded an opportunity from a high level in the organization for a positive content input.

There are even sadder flights from plain language, sadder because they are also flights from hard meanings. That there is no objection by his country to the employment of a certain man by the Organization becomes: 'a favourable advisory determination has been received'. In short, he has been politically cleared. I find it hard to believe that anyone uses such deodorized terminology straight, as though it were the simplest, most direct and intelligible way of saying what you mean. Nor can I bring myself to think it was seriously expected to deceive anybody; and, though it is verging on the sinister, it seems a long way from *1984*, from 'liquidated' and all those words. It seems—or maybe I'm just being hopeful—a mongrel, half out of routine, pompous governmental jargon, half out of plain embarrassment. So it joins hands on one side with the gobbledegook some governments still think is suitable formal expression, a sort of verbal morning-dress, and on the other

with the undertakers' range of clichés to avoid ever having to
say: 'He is dead'.

This extraordinarily elaborate, abstracted style, yet one full
of dead metaphors, soon becomes an organizational litany.
Listen to this and notice how much the prose creates a world of
its own, in which thought is castrated by conventionalized
phrasing. The prose moves, oozes, from one dead phrase to
another. It is like hopping on paving stones across a sluggish
river. I will italicize the paving stones:

> As two-thirds of the world's population are lagging
> behind *in the fight to secure* their *efficient co-operation*
> towards possible *social, economic and cultural welfare targets,*
> the *paramount importance* of the *human factor* in the develop-
> ment of these countries and *its promotion in all possible ways*
> is being *increasingly recognized* as a *primary goal* in the
> organization's *action in favour of* education, science and
> culture.
>
> In the *present project* great *importance will therefore be
> attached* to the *implementation of research* and studies *aimed
> at exploring* the *high relevance of strategies* of public policy
> in seeking *developmental goals* and the *significance* to these of
> *behaviouristic motivations* and *innovative patterns* in different
> *societal settings.*

That is from a pastiche created by a colleague of mine. No:
a patchwork or compilation, since all the phrases have been
used in agency documents, and so are true to their spirit. After
those early paragraphs the prose goes sliding along from stone
to stone in its all-too-predictable way; it is like being beaten
slowly into insensibility with cotton-wool. Redundancy, lack
of clarity, circumlocution have become defensive routines.
The pseudo-technical, impersonal jargon is chiefly protective.

The practice of simultaneous translation in four or five
languages highlights another difficulty, which comes from the
differences between languages. A speaker who is idiomatic,

E

concrete and metaphorical may be difficult to interpret simultaneously into French, for example. The French interpreter is likely to be left behind since he often has to make a metaphor into a discursive statement. With Russian it is different; the images, except where they draw on particular Westernized experiences (say, on the world of advertising), go easily into Russian. For the more earthy metaphors there is usually an equivalent.

There are almost as many styles in speechmaking as there are nations, but on the whole the more polite and flowery, the more elaborately-guarded, styles win. When in doubt use more and more formal politeness. In a world in which everyone is called a 'distinguished delegate' it is unlikely that anyone will act with inexcusable rudeness and put his foot through the drum.

There is some sense in this. National styles do differ and are easily misunderstood. So, irony, and especially the throwaway, self-mocking Anglo-Saxon kind, does not travel well. And gestures are certainly not international currency, except for those few, obvious, learned items of gestural lingua franca such as the handshake. Outside the Anglo-Saxon countries the gesture by which two statesmen, looking as though they only occasionally stand on two limbs, embrace one another from about a foot-and-a-half apart, each putting his arms out so as to touch the other man on the shoulders or at the sides of the chest, that gesture enshrined in a thousand airport reception photographs, is gaining ground.

So there is a pressure in international organizations to find a form of language which, though its users hope it says what has to be said, avoids unnecessary incidents, insoluble problems, time-wasting arguments, accusations of bias. Over one hundred and twenty nations have, almost literally speaking, over one hundred and twenty different styles. The pressure to find an 'esperanto style', one which has not too many unmanageable and unpredicted reverberations, is strong. The need to find something like a universal, uniform, accepted tone is part of the need to keep the inevitable political stresses within manageable bounds, so that the work of the organization in pursuing its non-political, shared ideals can go on.

Woolliness has sometimes to be resorted to so as to help keep the organization still talking, still getting some good things done. The direct and concrete in speech and writing at the wrong time; abrupt, unlubricated gestures which might be misunderstood by people of a different nationality from the speaker—such habits practised thoughtlessly may widen cracks in the fabric. There is a great deal of room for improvement in United Nations prose. But the vagueness and pussy-footing is sometimes a reflection of the pressures under which such organizations work, and apparently must work; and an attempt not to increase those pressures.

The pressures on language reflect the stresses in relationships: among the member states of the organization, between representatives of member states and what is called 'the Secretariat', the full-time officials, and among the officials themselves. Such pressures are inherent in the nature of the organizations. Everyone says on every suitable occasion: 'If the U.N. agencies didn't exist we would have to invent them'. That is probably true. But in any organization, anywhere, that phrase tends to be used when participants are even more than usually aware of the enormous nervous cost of maintaining it, and find themselves driven on to their uppers before they come up with, if they do manage to come up with, a final, inescapable justification.

In their public appearances, the representatives of member states tend to take up, sometimes apparently unconsciously, sometimes with an obvious histrionic relish and slightly larger than life, the roles they think are expected of them. They tend to play up to their own nation's stereotypes in the eyes of foreigners; or, trickier, try to embody their nation's own image of itself and project it towards other nations, in the hope that

they will accept it. In any long debate the mixture of compet-
ing and contrasting signals makes a rich, self-orchestrating
symphony. The English are as likely as not to open their
intervention with a half-serious, half-self-mocking: 'Of course,
to plain chaps like me . . .; after all, they don't really believe
they are as plain as they're making out. Spanish speakers from
Latin America use such elaborate rhetoric that the whole
performance seems unconsciously designed to show that even a
language whose rhetoric is highly-developed in its dramatic
native land, has been given, like church architecture, even more
superbly baroque qualities, after it has been transplanted and
employed for a few centuries in the even more dramatic air and
landscape of the Andes.

These are among the more playful levels of exchange. At a
serious, workaday, level one is struck by the formality of this
kind of diplomatic life. The necessary formality. It would
become unbearable if it were really meant, personally.

From outside, diplomatic manoeuvres always seem comical.
They often seem that way from the inside too, sometimes even
more so; but some also seem unavoidable, the only manner of
proceeding. The duty of national officials is to carry out as
fully as they can the briefs given to them by their governments.
Some diplomats are as much of a pain-in-the-neck as any self-
involved and over-insistent individual is, but even imaginative
and fair-minded diplomats argue their briefs hard.

No doubt many of them find parts of their work painful,
even hard on their consciences. For most diplomats the formal
theatrical styles of diplomatic life are a saving process; and
preserve also the possibility of personal relationships with others
outside official business. They know the modes and they expect
their hearers to know them too. They are not much deceived
in themselves and would be startled if their hearers were. So
on the whole things are saved; though you are bound to wonder
how long that kind of thing can go on before you lose the sense
that there is a real self inside.

The staff of the organization, too, have to learn to care and not to care. For them it is on the whole easier. They are trying to keep a balance, and an open area. They are not promoters of a line but servants of an idea on behalf of the organization's ruling bodies. In such circumstances they too need to learn certain formal movements because those movements are understood and speedy. Which is not at all to say that when a stand has to be made on some clear issue of principle you are without means. Such moments do occur, and you can then be plain and firm. For other occasions, you learn the useful conventions. It seems silly to see yourself, looking down for a moment through the eyes of your alter ego as it hangs from the ceiling, politely refusing an invitation to a small, private dinner party, which you have been told has been arranged in your honour but which might well have political implications and so be misused by one side or another: your own presence, that is, might be misused as political evidence. It is odd to see yourself doing that; but not, after all, difficult. These are special kinds of relationships and not really personal at all.

You may build up a strong impression that someone,—an ambassador of a member state, say—by the recurrence or insistence or spin of some of his requests is trying you out, testing how far he can get you to go along the line laid down by his particular brief. If you are both new, there is bound to be much jockeying to see where your line might be weak. It is engaging to think that it would always help to tell him straight. No doubt it would be relieving. But I doubt if it would usually do much good. Flat-out statements would as likely as not be misunderstood; frank man-to-man talk looks to many people of other cultures insufferably rude and crude. The attempt at frankness might uselessly set back negotiations, since if the message—'don't try undue pressures'—were taken as nakedly as that, it would be at once rejected; no doubt in formal terms, but no less vigorously for that. Still, the conventions are to hand and on the whole are effective. Once you have decided that what is going on has become unwarranted you can, formally and politely, without heat but without misunderstanding or arguing, indicate that this is so. There is no need for apologies, or half-promises of generosity in the future or other emollients. You may feel piqued that he has thought you the sort of person on whom that kind of thing might be tried, but you know he is testing the limits of the ground in accordance with the forms of his diplomatic game; so you are not really angry. You are not engaged in that kind of way. It is all a kind of play. But in another sense it is serious, serious playing.

Sometimes there can be a sort of beauty, the effect of an elegant dance, about such movements. I remember once having to take formal notice as Acting Director-General of UNESCO of an important and very serious announcement an ambassador was to make on behalf of his government. Everyone involved played his necessary part. The notice was given in the terms required, the elements of the response had been considered beforehand and were given in exact terms too; and the meeting ended after only a few minutes, with hardly a redundant syllable. It had to be like that.

Then a strange thing happened. The ambassador relaxed, his face and indeed his whole physical appearance changed, as though his body had been brushed over by a light breeze. He turned, shook hands with us all and made a few personal remarks. He knew most of the people there as individuals, and they knew and liked him, as a person. The change, the lift in the atmosphere, was remarkable. And so, quite quickly, he left the room. I was intrigued by the whole operation and had a strong sense of having been there before. Where else was it that you felt the atmosphere change so suddenly, from that of a necessary, set, public ritual to direct personal relationships? After a while I remembered and laughed. It was a certain moment after a working-class funeral in the North of England, not long after you are back in the house from the cemetery, and the tea and sandwiches have been passed round. There too the atmosphere suddenly changes, lifts. People begin to talk about family things, about what each of them, and others who aren't there, are doing now. The working-class event is much more complex than the diplomatic. But there are clear similarities; both switch suddenly from acting out a public ritual to a relaxed meeting.

In the nature of their jobs, staff members of international organizations themselves have special problems in relationships. They are, to begin with, uprooted from more than a hundred different national cultures and living, most of them, in a foreign culture, perhaps a very foreign culture indeed. Or, if it is argued that they do not fully live in the culture of their organization's host country (but if they have children that is difficult to avoid), let us say they are living within an international group or professional sub-culture which doesn't express the national style of any one of them. Some may, as the years go by, find it difficult to think of going back home; their children or wives have thoroughly settled in the once foreign environment; their salaries are much higher than they could hope to get at home; their home-towns or capital cities look from this distance unbearably provincial or flat; some may know they cannot go home, to a new government which has taken power since they left, and be likely to remain out of prison or highly uncomfortable exile in a far province.

So the nervous cost of this kind of work varies enormously according to where you come from. For almost all members of the organization's staff it is a complex situation and can produce a whole range of unpleasant practices, such as excessive visa-hunting (making doubly sure that someone above you has initialled all your items of work so that, in case of unpleasant repercussions, the buck has been passed); or the self-congratulatory inflation of reports after missions abroad; or the great battery of don't-rock-the-boat, *noli-me-tangere* attitudes which show themselves, as much as anywhere, in the tendency to write excessively adulatory, or at least excessively guarded and on-the-one-hand-on-the-other, performance reports on your subordinates, or in the all-pervading marsh-gas of gossip about everything under the sun, but most often about sexual peccadilloes or petty peculation, neither of which are anything like as common as the gossip implies; or in the difficulty of making jokes, other than in the bosom of your own family, about any aspect of the organization, since almost all jokes might be taken to imply criticisms of someone, somewhere, in the apparatus. Above all, you soon learn to stop making jokes at cocktail parties, even though they may not be jokes about particular people and may be pretty well on the mark, unmalicious and quite funny. You stop after you have noticed that at such moments a shutter or film comes over the face of your listener, a trapped look. You have put him in a spot he didn't wish to be in. He doesn't want that kind of relationship. He takes a quick look round, for an escape route or simply to gain time so as to avoid having to react directly to the joke. To do so might seem to imply agreement to a criticism, or commitment to a point of view.

These are among the costs of living in a hothouse community which can assume little, which has few automatic habits and assumptions to work from day-by-day, which can take very little for granted. So the administrative regulations for the personnel of international organizations have to be spelled out in more detail than those of most national organizations. Take a typical, large, British professional organization. It is likely to allow a member of staff a day off for a family funeral, because that is part of the culture's practice, part of the patterns of respect built into the culture's organizations. One goes to family funerals; they do not happen often, and on the whole people don't falsely claim a death in the family so as to get a free day off. If it did happen often, there would have to be precise rules; that it doesn't happen often is shown by the fact that the exceptions are enshrined in one of the culture's more hoary jokes, about the office boy asking to be allowed to go to his grandmother's funeral on the day of the cup-tie replay. We can make jokes about the exceptions, because they are exceptions.

Shared cultural assumptions make that degree of free play possible. Perhaps not always in really large organizations, where the pressure for exact rules must be stronger. But here is one interesting instance of adaptability. The BBC, I believe, and, for all I know, some other large organizations, automatically gives two extra days' leave a year to each employee to allow for the incidence of grandmother's funerals or family weddings or what have you. They are called 'bisques', by analogy from, I believe, the name for a free shot in croquet. They show a cultural ritual, grandmother's funeral, enshrined and institutionalized.

But how can you establish that degree of freedom in an international organization whose employees come from many widely-different cultures? How many such special occasions can you allow for, given the range of different customs as to religion, family, national piety? How many funerals a year would you allow to staff members from cultures where the extended family has a strong hold? How can you ensure that any arrangements which seem reasonably tolerant of variety are not, because of their very tolerance, abused? Not all nations have the same views on how far you may exploit whatever areas of movement have been left within a system laid down by a superior authority. How, in short, do you ensure that you do not end with a system which admits and codifies all the main elements of uncodified freedom, indulgences, in each member state's separate system but which recognizes and obeys none of those assumed constraints, inherited checks and balances, each separate state can to some extent rely on? You can only avoid that unworkable result by, first, making sure the terms of service are generous on all reasonable grounds, and then by laying them out as exactly as possible so that the areas for multiple interpretation and over-interpretation are reduced to a minimum. It is one of the prices of belonging to *no* culture, in your professional life.

In day-to-day relations with other members of the staff there are difficult problems of tone to be negotiated. Your first shock is realizing what a big job lies ahead in trying to understand and be understood other than thinly, how much your own culture's ways of making contact are not necessarily transferable. Even more, realizing how closed our previous world has been, even within our own culture. British academics do not much meet British businessmen; arts academics do not greatly mix with medicals. We find for ourselves and then help sustain, within our national culture, that smaller society whose signals we learn intimately. We join it and shut the door after us.

So to join a large international organization is doubly unsettling; it severs you from particular cultural signals and it pitches you in with new types of people and types of minds—scientists, lawyers, politicians, journalists, technicians and, most unusual of all, high-level manipulators, tough, shrewd, effective but with little regard for principle as a primary consideration.

Many of the stresses I have described are met in too much of a self-preserving way, and I don't underestimate the fact that many people bend badly under the pressures. Still, when that has been admitted, one remembers other considerations: that those defensive reactions arise as often as not from the exceptional painfulness of making some critical decisions in such an environment. Where so many are so cut off it can be exceptionally difficult to make certain personal decisions about members of staff; in a settled environment they would be, though still painful, more easily borne. One remembers also that the big pressures sometimes meet heroic responses. I am not thinking now of direct political pressures. I mean, for one thing, the stress that can be put upon an intelligent and sensitive and honest Asian, deeply committed to his own culture but also committed to the ideals for which the organization stands, seeing his wife and children becoming steadily more Westernized, feeling himself inevitably getting out of touch with his own roots, which may mean, in such a case, losing his sense of a different rhythm of life from that which the West offers and a rhythm he feels in his bones is nearer the truth; to face this strain on the conscience from the contrasting pulls of your new international profession and your duty to your homeland is to risk a profound personal disorientation.

Then you remember another submerged, unlegislated role of the fulltime staff—one I've hinted at already. It is not much talked about, but the staff have to recognize its trickiness if they are to do their proper job. This is an extension of their duty to help their ruling bodies keep the dialogue open, to avoid unnecessary strains on the system which might cause a breakdown. Here, as so often, the staff have a double role. They have to be neutral, keeping open for others the areas for useful negotiation; they can also find themselves pushed into a more positive role, because they have occasionally to act as counterweights. The organization embodies the idea that national states will pay their homage and their dues to the intellect and the imagination above national considerations, to certain values and standards outside particular national needs. It is a remarkable ideal, and it is remarkable that it still works at all. But it is necessarily always under pressure because, as I've already said, member states are political organisms and their Ministries are more concerned with the national interest than with maintaining agreed standards for the intellectual life. Mind: they vary a lot in the degree to which they push their national interest; some are blatant. So there is a built-in loss of efficiency in executing the programmes of international organizations. A great deal of effort has to be diverted into insuring against objections from any one of a hundred-and-twenty-odd member states, on the grounds that one of their gods has been insulted.

Their peculiar position leads members of the staff, in their effort to maintain neutrality so that the job can be done, towards sometimes becoming the keepers of the organization's conscience. Not all of them, I should say. Some members of staff don't try to be international civil servants; in any important issue they work for their own countries. Overdone, this conscience-keeping role would be bad for both the organization and the staff. Since many of the staff joined the organization because they do believe in its ideals, they need to be particularly self-critical here. Still, the staff have from time to time to hold the line until member states have got back to working relations among themselves. The line has to be held, also, so that the respect of the international intellectual world, a different entity from the grouping of member states but crucial to such an institution as UNESCO, is retained. That respect is easily lost and, once lost, would have taken with it the organization's chief claim to distinctiveness. If you are involved with questions of peace, of human rights, of education, of the intellectual and artistic life in general, you have got to be seen to be, at least more often than not, both competent and free. At what point does 'accommodation', made so as to keep the organization afloat and still talking, become a fatal letting-go of those very intellectual ideals which the organization was set up to exemplify and serve.

There is an interesting feature of such organizations; I mean organizations which have these two characteristics in common apart from bigness: that they have to do with intellectual and artistic matters, and that they are exposed to political forces. This feature is the existence inside the organizations themselves of a moral litmus paper, a group of people who are assumed to be free from the pressures of ideologies but shrewd, the highly-skilled practitioners of a difficult craft.

On to such a group there tends to be fathered the job of judging how well the organization is living up to its own high purposes. They are regarded as the godlike but shrewd communal eye within, the trapped spectators. That they are technicians is felt to ensure that their judgements will be not only intelligent but honest: they are straight men; they have stayed out of the main rat-race.

In large international organizations this role is given to the interpreters who sit in their glass-fronted sound-proof boxes hour after hour and day after day, interpreting unemotionally whatever comes up through the wires from the debating floor. 'Even the interpreters were impressed' is one of the highest forms of praise about a speaker. It is felt to be not simply praise for skill or virtuosity; it suggests that, since the interpreters are assumed to be unerringly able to recognize humbug when they see it, they are impressed only by virtues proper to the place and its ideals. The translators, who are not even seen behind glass but work wholly in the background, are felt to have similar powers.

Much the same role is played by the sound engineers in radio and the camera men in television, and is expressed in such phrases as: 'Even the engineers were listening hard' or, the best test for a television comedy show: 'Even the cameramen were laughing'. The cameramen and the engineers, like the interpreters, might well, after all, have been bored stiff; the implication is that they usually are, even though they go on turning in a good professional job; they have to look and listen for hours on end without making any personal interventions; they foresee and suffer all. If they, then, are impressed by a certain performance, who else could fail to be? Of course, there is something ritualistic and mythical about these attributions; they tell you much more about the pressures within the institutions which create the myths than about the critical abilities of sound engineers or cameramen or interpreters or translators, shrewd though they all may be.

The stresses of working in an international organization come, I've argued, partly from the delicacy of your relations to member states but, more deeply, from the difficulty of making contact in a context which has no cultural coherence. No doubt some people will think the difficulty exaggerated. Surely, they will ask, there are international communities already; for instance, of scientists? I do not think so. There are certainly some groups, of scientists and other specialists, who know each other across national boundaries. They know each other *as scientists and specialists*. They form international, professional sub-cultures. But these are relatively thin and two-dimensional cultures. They have common international professional languages; outside that, they get along well enough at what you might call the level of international acquaintance-ship.

The gains from international work can include larger perspectives, a chance to reduce some of your parochialism, a sharper sense of other cultures and of your own, and a sharper sense too of the need to find common ground for speaking across cultures and without benefit of a sustaining shared society. Presumably more and more people are going to find themselves in such situations. Whatever else they achieve, and whatever their weaknesses, their doubts and limitations, today's international organizations are testing the ways in which we can be genuine, speak straight, be in touch without the adventitious help of belonging by birth, without benefit of shared jokes, silences, gestures or 'bisques'.

V

PRIVATE FACES IN PUBLIC PLACES

V

Private Faces in Public Places

In this lecture I am going to talk about large-scale public communication; about broadcasting, and mostly about television, the most massive of the mass media. The first fact of life for broadcasting is that it is never left to go its own way. Since all countries believe broadcasting has special qualities they all take collective social decisions about its use. Those decisions define the structure of the broadcasting systems themselves, the attention given to politics, religion, minority groups, the part played by the provinces or regions as against the capital or nation as a whole, public accountability in financial or in programme affairs. Those decisions define the amount of censorship, the role given to commerce and the nature of competition, if there is any. They define also the prevailing style of each system; light or heavy or something of both. It is plain that from a study of their formal arrangements for broadcasting alone you can go a long way towards analysing the different natures of societies, warts and all.

With most countries, after an analysis like that, you are more aware of the warts than of the beauty marks. It would be depressing to start from that end. I will instead sketch the sort of connections between broadcasting and society which could best serve those views of the individual's relations to his culture which lay behind my first four lectures; and then I will look at the main obstacles to such connections. In other words, this will be a sort of ideal, as seen by me. It would get short shrift in most parts of the world.

First, a broadcasting system ought to reflect the culture in which it lives. Which sounds easy. But what aspects of the culture? Whose view of the culture? That of a dominant cultivated class? Or that which commercial entrepreneurs think their mass consumers want or ought to have? And for what purpose is that view being promoted? To support the prevailing political or commercial ideology? If control is tight and highly centralized, which can happen in multi-party democracies as well as in monolithic states—because control can be exercised in other ways than by official orders—the contours of the culture will not be reflected in broadcasting; they will be flattened out.

It follows that broadcasters should be free to be diverse, open to more than one way of seeing the culture they live in. Broadcasters have to ask harder than most of us whether prevailing ways of seeing their society are adequate. If they don't, they will get a great deal wrong, beginning with the very tones in which they speak to people. When the tones are wrong that usually indicates that the grasp is wrong.

All societies are always changing, and probably especially quickly today. It is always difficult to analyse such changes and even more difficult to decide your attitude towards them. But certainly mass media, if they are to reflect a society adequately, must try to reflect the changes going on within it, not only show it as it is today, as if it were finished and set. Most societies forever argue within themselves; with, roughly speaking, those who want change on one side and those who want to maintain the established order on the other. It is always a confused battle, fought on many fronts and on many levels, and with slogans doing duty most of the time for serious discussion. Think of the difficulty of making sense of the argument about the permissive society in Britain as they are filtered through most of the usual outlets. That label alone begs most of the questions, and gets argument off on the wrong foot. Broadcasters should be free to provide a platform for people to hear such arguments better and to join in.

The case for diversity has a trickier side: that freedom for each of us ought to include the opportunity to change or widen our tastes if we wish. Our backgrounds, our educations, our working lives all tend to make us set within certain ranges of taste. The provision made for us is almost always along these fixed lines though varied by class, background etc.; it is easier, more predictable, economically more worthwhile to do that; and soon these lines come to seem like facts of nature to us. I am not saying simply that poorly-educated people are catered for with a driving, taste-setting precision; though that is by and large true. But by implication it gives too much credit to the tastes of other groups within society. We are back once again with the inadequacy of most ways of talking about taste. We all have a great deal to learn about other styles of life.

'Widening', 'diversifying', still sound too feature-less and relativistic. In broadcasting organizations there is certainly a tendency to think that simply to make more things available is not only a necessary but a sufficient and un-edited activity. This is a myth, since choices are being made all the time by the broadcasters; but one can see how the attitude arises. There is a powerful resistance within British culture as a whole to making distinctions, recognizing different standards, choosing between, saying you think some things better than others; and it weighs particularly heavily on those who work in the mass media. 'The Beatles are as good as Beethoven' is the quickest short-hand for that attitude.

But it won't do. It would be daft to beat the Beatles about the head because they are not Beethoven. In a way which did not seem possible ten or twelve years ago, they caught some aspects of the culture of young people; they are far ahead of the popular songwriters who came before them. That is a gain; and from it you can make distinctions between kinds of popular music, according to its liveliness, its inventiveness and so on.

But that is to make judgements, and once started you can't put an artificial limit to the process. To claim that 'they're both authentic', may say something about the Beatles and

Beethoven, but is not the last word. To imply from it that the two are, in all important senses, as good as each other is to give up thinking. Some works of art attempt more and demand more than others; where they succeed their achievement is greater than others. So broadcasters have to think about their choices. Why shouldn't more of us have more chance to hear these good, these better, things?

If broadcasters, then, are to avoid being merely reflectors (which in most countries means reflectors of someone-in-power's idea of what the culture should look like), if they are going to express the movement towards change in their societies, if they are to widen our options, if they are to carry out their inescapable making of choices thoughtfully and independently, if broadcasters are to do all this they will be critically involved, a sort of yeast in society. They will be active agents of change. This disturbs the conventionally minded and angers many politicians. It is not popular in any country. Of course, in some countries there is no real problem; the broadcasters are not allowed to risk being risky. Elsewhere, they can hardly settle for less, if they are to meet the medium's possibilities.

One good test of whether broadcasters have this sort of freedom is whether young people of talent feel encouraged to join television because it looks like giving them a chance to develop their particular gifts. If one network is dominated by, stamped with the views of, ideologues or another by fast-buck seekers, those are signs that the medium's possibilities have been narrowed. A good structure attracts people with a great variety of talents, whether to inform, educate or entertain; it has at its centre people who feel that the medium is a new kind of medium and can do new and different things—that drama, and the treatment of news, and comedy and exposition will on television be different from their former selves. These basic truths are not even glimpsed, let alone honoured, in many countries.

New forms; and new audiences, new kinds of audience. One characteristic reinforces the other. Most people in a television audience have never seen and never will see a West End play. They have no set expectations; the dramatist and producer are imaginatively free, within the technical possibilities and the limits of their new medium; free to invoke new audiences. It is always interesting to assess the implied respect of a television writer for the capacities of his unknown audience. But to respect in this sense is to have a fundamentally different outlook from that which says; 'Here is the same old West End audience' or 'Here is an unknown mass I want to amuse, woo, capture; or 'Here is a mass whose ideology I want to reinforce'. It says instead 'Here is a medium whose technical possibilities are fascinating; and its audiences do not necessarily expect the established forms in art, or education or information; nor do they have habitual responses'. This combination of interest in the medium itself with interest in reaching new kinds of audiences has been responsible for some of the distinctive successes of television. No system which prevents that combination is worth much.

To sum up, the necessary conditions are: a structure that doesn't interfere politically, that gives many kinds of artistic and intellectual ability room to manoeuvre, that implies the medium is more than an inert channel, that respects possible audiences and doesn't try to make them into a homogeneous mass down whose throat things are pushed. Conditions such as these are likely to show that the medium has more possibilities and its audiences greater capacities than we had imagined in advance.

Most nations are not going to set up conditions anywhere near those I have just described. Some will simply not relinquish straight political control, though not all will call it that; euphemisms are easy to find; others will not relinquish the profit that comes from tying the media to the ends of selling. How to alter things? Some sort of revolution? That's unlikely in Britain, and anyway the final condition of mass communications after most revolutions has been no better than the earlier. Still, there is a chance, if we take thought better, of getting more elbow room in some countries.

It is a big if. Most public debate on communications in Britain is poor. There is some good cultural criticism but it is not known to most politicians. That is one area where thought does not much irrigate the corridors of power; as I learned when I served on the Pilkington Committee on Broadcasting, and found that the long debate on the effects of advertising in commercial democracies was unknown to some men who were involved at very high levels with the question of advertising in a public medium. I do not mean operators in advertising; I mean public servants with more than commercial responsibilities. And I do not imply that they should have accepted any particular position. They should have known the lines of the argument, though. So on the one hand commercial pressures have an easy victory because the defences are ill-thought out; on the other, the suspicions of many politicians are so strong you wonder whether their professions of belief in the free play of argument are only lip-service, because based on inadequate thinking-through of what those fine phrases will mean in practice, in hurt pride and rocked pedestals. Then the commercial people, who are likely (being in the image business themselves) to be more deferential to public figures and their images than the non-commercial, make common cause with the politicians in their approach to broadcasting; and we are set on a course miles away from the one I am arguing for.

Is the situation more cheerful if one turns to the more intellectual politicians? Not much. One or two exceptions gratefully admitted, one is as likely as not to fall here into the pit of relativist high-jinks. I remember a high-ranking politician discussing the Pilkington Report and, in particular, its attempt to steer between the false lights of 'giving the people what the people want' and 'giving the people what they ought to have'. He enjoyed himself no end showing how broad-minded and unstuffy and unhighbrow he was, by refusing to recognize that broadcasters had any problems in the choices they made in programming; and he finally produced the unforgettable sentence: 'I stand up for the common man's right to be trivial if he pleases'.

You could see behind the smart phrasing what he thought a strong and necessary assertion. This is really what freedom means, he was implying: that men shall be free to go to Hell or Heaven in their own way; the liberal tradition is still strong, still good. Bravo. So far. But as a response to the actual situation within competitive broadcasting it was ludicrous: the pressure to trivialize serious things, the trivial material relentlessly produced, the unspoken but clear assumption that most people are capable of responding to very little; in short, the lack of any substantial freedom at any point in the process for the common man, except the final freedom to switch off, which is a bit like telling a man in prison that he is at least free to kill himself. One saw in that politician a failure to realize all this, an ignoring of the possibilities of the medium, an easy settling for epigrams as a substitute for thought, a failure to see that a man's 'right' must start with the right not to have his range of choice prematurely narrowed; one saw, finally, an unconscious contempt for the abilities of the very people the man flattered himself he was speaking in support of.

At least he was interested enough in broadcasting to want to talk about it, and most politicians are not. Which makes it difficult to get the debate improved. Still, in some of the countries where commercial pressures hardly exist and where the politicians have decided that broadcasting *is* important, usually on the wrong grounds, the situation is worse and the freedom less. In such countries it is not permitted, and certainly not through the public media, to express views counter to the orthodoxy, except for a few aunt sallies or clay pigeons of ideas. This position is justified by any number of arguments, from the crude to the complicated. Societies such as these have sometimes been helped to arrive at their present ideology by the work of powerful critical currents opposing the then prevailing ideologies. They were at work both under and above ground, since it was then much more difficult to centralize and control the distribution of information. It would be almost impossible for a critical dialogue to get substantially launched above ground in those countries today. Regimes which were set up after intense argument can now close the gates on themselves and, by a combination of total control of the communications media and new devices for surveillance, prohibit effective debate about their own set-up, outside small face-to-face groups.

That is one way of keeping broadcasting in jail. Another is to claim it must be free to meet public taste but to tie it tightly to commerce which, for its own purposes, must define public taste in a thinned-down way. In between the two, and sharing some of the qualities of each, are certain societies in which broadcasting looks freer but is by all sorts of invisible constraints bound to a static and out-of-date view of what the particular cultural heritage is.

Small wonder that high hopes are put in those developments which can make many more outlets available. Then, the argument goes, it will be possible to serve a great number of small and different groups at the same time and cheaply. Broadcasting will be on a local scale; it will be something people take part in, not something they are simply given; it will serve numbers of overlapping groups; areas of different sizes and types (rural, urban, suburban, mountain, seashore, etc.) will have their own stations, and so will different kinds of professional or recreational or religious or artistic or intellectual interest. All will operate by and for themselves, for their own kinds of people and for any others who care to listen; and no one will interfere with anyone else. The hands of the centralized controller will lie idle; there will be no place for him, thank goodness.

It is the hand-press or small-holding dream of communications, and it is an engaging dream. I hope something like that can come about; it would have many virtues. Minorities of all kinds are not well enough served by broadcasters today; their case almost always goes by default. Still, small-scale provision, no matter how useful in itself, will do little to solve the problems I have been describing, and may make them worse. Incidentally, in those countries where there is no public access to the use of the present centralized media it is utopian to think the authorities will let people lay their hands on the gear which would make small-group broadcasting possible. That would be like giving everyone his own automatic rifle.

Even in less controlled societies small-scale provision will not solve the big problems. First, because however much local and specialized communication you may have, there is and will remain a clear need for good communication at the national level and beyond. That will always be needed as part of a society's dialogue with itself *as a whole*. One of the benefits of broadcasting is exactly that it allows a nation to speak to itself, and nation to speak to nation, if they wish. It is a reversion to parochialism to think small-scale communication is a substitute for large-scale; the two kinds are complementary.

Admittedly, as I've said, the national dialogues we have now are not usually effective. But, and this is the second objection to thinking of small-scale broadcasting as a cure-all, if we stop caring about the better use of the national channels because we have put all our trust in the small-scale we shall have handed those national channels over all the more firmly to the very people we criticize, the ideological toughs and the commercial sharp-shooters, so that they can distort them for their own ends. We shall have allowed those people, by letting us have small-scale broadcasting to play with, to divide and rule. Variety on the small-scale will have been bought by forfeiting significant links and critical involvement with power, authority and the main currents within society. It will not then matter how many dialogues go on in that patchwork of smaller units: the heavyweight stuff will be controlled more tightly than ever. Finally, large-scale broadcasting gives the broadcasters opportunities to extend their medium which are different from those of small-scale work; they need both.

Broadcasters ought to be given the greatest possible freedom, so long as they meet these basic criteria: that they are in touch with their culture; that they have thought about the responsibilities of the medium as well as felt its interest, and that they come under regular scrutiny of the right kind.

To take the last first. Public scrutiny is necessary; but it needs to be more carefully thought about than most proposals made today. Establish a large, watchdog, committee with representatives from all parts of society, postmen as well as Vice-Chancellors, trade unionists as well as Head-mistresses of independent day schools, and you will find that such a body has to be too large to have effective teeth. Establish a smaller one and you have divided responsibility between them and your Board of Governors; and they, in debates about the B.B.C., are usually presumed to continue to exist. By both procedures you will have diffused the responsibility of the broadcasters themselves and provided yet another buffer between them and the play of public opinion. You will have established a corporate mule, inorganic in its relationship to the profession, unprofessional in just the ways that matter here, a committee which will baffle the best-intentioned broadcasters by the self-cancelling nature of its debates and advice, and which the not-so-well disposed broadcasters will be able to play with, both ends against the middle, whilst they sit on the side-lines smiling politely till the watchdogs go home.

To be effective, scrutiny of broadcasters has to be closer, better informed and more various. Committees, yes; of several kinds. To begin with, a core of specialist committees which, though they do not have executive powers, are so well-informed in their fields and in broadcating's relations to them that no broadcaster can safely ignore them and most won't want to. In fact, several of those committees exist already in the United Kingdom though one hears too little about their activities. Then, more of the direct play of public opinion: a much better range of criticism in the Press, more attention to 'communications and culture' in the universities and elsewhere; and more attention to them in the schools, not as threats to high culture but as inescapable features of contemporary society which can work well or badly. All in all, we need a more varied, well-informed range of public scrutinies going on all the time.

What being in touch with the culture means I spoke about earlier. Its main characteristics are refusing to accept a restricted view of the society, being sensitive to its variety, being responsive to change, to possibilities beyond what appear on the surface today: the society's possibilities, the medium's possibilities and the possibilities of the people who make up his audiences. There should be a good level of cultural literacy throughout any broadcasting organization, but it should be especially strong, conscious and articulate at the top. Senior administrators need that sort of understanding if they are to give a wide range of talents sufficient freedom of the right kind; and so as to fend off, on the right grounds and with the necessary energy, the pressures to politicize and commercialize their medium; it will also make them more willing and able to meet justified criticism straight, without flannelling or evading. This is worth stressing because broadcasters can be smug and Olympian. They work in an important medium; there are few of them and they know they have great influence—they control the few channels which serve millions of people. But Olympian attitudes are wholly unjustified. The controllers ought instead to be on their knees asking for guidance. If they do not have a well-nourished sense of their culture they will add rigidity to their smugness. If they have not thought about the inevitable acts of censorship their work entails they will be blind censors.

Blind censors with rigid imaginations. To be a censor is unavoidable; to be a blind censor is inexcusable. 'Censor' is a deliberately strong word. I do not mean open political or any other of the obvious kinds of censorship. I mean that, since the available channels and the available hours are few, every decision to put something on is taken in the light of many more decisions, most of them not brought to the level of consciousness, *not* to put a lot of other things on.

By what criteria are the choices made? First, they are partially defined by the culture; second, they are limited by the structure within which the broadcasters are made to work; third, they are rationalized by the broadcasters themselves in professional terms of art. You don't put on free debate in certain countries; you explain that people don't want it and would regard it as rude. You don't put on minority drama in other countries; you explain that it would be against public taste and that people can tell phoniness when they see it. If you are a controller up against a wall defending yourself, you explain that when it really comes down to it there aren't all that many good ideas for programmes, only about enough to go round. Above all, you resort to your professional terms of art. This is true of all forms of large-scale publishing, the Press and films as much as broadcasting. All recoil from the word 'censor'. 'I choose by my news sense', says a typical Western journalist. 'I simply know what my audience will think an interesting feature', says another. 'I can tell a good TV programme when I see it; that's all', says a producer. All these remarks carry the sense of belonging to a mystery, imply that each of the large-scale media has peculiar qualities which interest and attract men to work in it. True. But those answers are also ways of refusing to recognize the prior limits imposed on the very definition of 'a good TV idea', or 'news', or an 'interesting' feature, imposed by the given ideas of any culture and the structures it has made for its public media.

In my experience, most people who work in those media

do not recognize the power of these influences behind their terms of art; they take the terms as absolute statements about universal and objective characteristics of their trade. Not to recognize this cultural colouring or these structural biases is to become an unwitting prisoner of the culture and the structure. Your choices, your rejections and your acceptances, will be forced on you from below and within, even whilst you are thinking yourself a free and easy rider in the medium. You may well be a success, because you may have a natural sense of what your culture most wants and what the structure will most allow you to exploit. But you will be missing the big opportunities. This is blind censorship, censorship by blind omission. It is not as sinister as political censorship, but it is stupid. We all need irrigating, and men in the media need it more than most of us.

So we come to the most difficult aspect of all: that broadcasters are morally involved with their societies. This relationship is hard to define but cannot be slipped away from. The life of the medium is not wholly internal to the medium. Still, it is very important to say, before looking into what the phrase means, that the broadcasters' moral involvement with the life of their society will only be well-faced if they first like their medium for itself. If the terms of moral involvement are expressed in too literal a way they become moralistic, which is the error of most watchdog bodies. To begin with, broadcasters have to be drawn to the medium for its own sake, not because they want either to do good to society or to subvert it. They should select themselves for the work. Without that, even their sense of moral involvement will be thin and too literal.

In talking about moral involvement I am deliberately using an old-fashioned form of words. A quite violent reaction was caused by a sentence in the Pilkington Report on broadcasting which argued that broadcasters had to recognize that they have:

A constant and living engagement with the moral condition of society.

None of us on the committee had a special interest in keeping
that particular form of words. No doubt there are better ways
of putting the point. We did have an interest in keeping the
idea. The fact that it ran against one of the great inhibitions of
the time didn't make it less worth saying. The Report was not
talking about the conscious promoting of some particular
ethical norms, or about moralizing. It was saying that broadcasters cannot settle for a wholly aesthetic definition of their
work. From the day they select the subject of their first programme, from the way they prepare and produce that programme, they are at every step involved with, meshed in with,
reinforcing or undermining, the value-systems of their society.
Though they may never give the matter a passing thought, the
pattern of their omissions and commissions, their repetitions
and gaps, the way they let the camera linger or switch it quickly,
the plays they choose and those they don't choose, the subjects
they select for discussion and the ways they produce those
discussions, the clothing they give their actors and actresses,
the sorts of interiors they order from the stage-designers—
all this will be engaged at all points with existing views of the
good life within their societies. There is no way out. They will,
to the extent that they are powerful at their work, be disposing
some people towards changes in directions they, the broadcasters, have consciously or unconsciously chosen.

So we might as well know better where we are. It would be
pleasant to be able to say that a broadcaster can resolve the
dilemma by balancing all sides, letting all sides appear with
reasonable regularity; and to some extent that is a fair aim. It
needs a considerable responsiveness to the culture as a whole,
and it is only partially possible, simply because there will still
have to be more omissions than acceptances. By what criteria
will the acceptances be made? On the frequency or force with

which certain attitudes come up? That seems mechanical. On their newness and novelty? That seems frivolous. Acceptances against the main stream will presumably have to be made, if we are to remain sensitive to change. On what grounds will the exceptions be chosen, for there are always more possibilities than one has time to cater for? Yours, because you are, you hope, an imaginative producer? Fine, but recognize that you are walking on the water. By what arguments would you justify this or that particular extension of the conventionally-accepted boundaries in, say, sexual explicitness? Because you think the conventional boundaries in your culture too restrictive? You may be right. But *there's* a large moral judgement for you. Because it makes an exciting programme, is 'good telly'? Wow! Because most people have by now got used to that kind of thing in the cinema? So the cinema sets the pace for broadcasting? Because everybody's doing it now? They are doing much else; why did you choose sexual explicitness? How do you answer those who claim that, in thus helping to push the boundaries further, you are damaging something important to the quality of the culture. Can you always and automatically dismiss such arguments as old-womanish? From all of which, and I could go on till I was out of breath, it is easy to see that, without at all being a do-gooder, a broadcaster is in all his decisions involved with the moral life of his society, with its patterns of values, with the stresses and changes those patterns of values are undergoing at any particular time. This kind of engagement has to be recognized if broadcasters are to do justice to their own cultures and to the capacities of the individuals who make up their audiences.

VI

A COMMON GROUND

G

VI

A Common Ground

These lectures have been about 'culture and communication', though I have avoided that phrase as the main title because it sounds too abstract and specialist. They have been about our common life and the quality of that life. And there's another phrase, the quality of life, which embarrasses some people and is carelessly used by others but can't easily be done without. A culture will always produce a picture of the world and ask its people to approve that picture and the values which stem from it. So to talk about the quality of a society's life is not, as some people seem to assume, to produce a sort of slide-rule of externally-verified, desirable values and measure the society against them. It is to look and listen, to ask what values are encouraged within a society, what discouraged; what the society allows in behaviour and standards without a risk for the individual of being rejected or of great nervous strain; how the society's patterns of values are changing. When you are trying to understand the quality of a society's life you are listening to much more than words, than its manifest assertions. You are trying to interpret and make into a coherent whole, as the society does, its attitudes to children, to death, to ambition, to the old, to the individual conscience, to foreigners, to the sick, to learning, to leisure, to the arts, to the search for truth, to privacy, and so on. We never make contact in the void. By all kinds of means we express to others and to ourselves a sense of relationships with the values of our culture, our general acceptance of them, or our rejections, or our simply taking-for-granted.

It would be pleasant to think that all the talk about communication today reflected and respected this diversity and

richness, but it rarely does. 'Communications' has become a
catch-word, a kind of cult-word. Obviously, our means of
passing information of one sort or another from one place to
another virtually instantaneously, to hundreds of millions, all
this has developed with almost unbelievable speed and effectiveness in the last couple of decades. So what then? Are we really
more in touch? A great many people, some out of technical
enthusiasm, some out of *naïveté*, some because they can tell a
good band-wagon when they see one, assure us that modern
communications will soon dispel all doubts. We may be
inclined to ask: 'where is the knowledge we have lost in information'; but, they say, we will soon see technological
marvels which are just around the corner recreate what they are
likely to call 'significant contacts one with another'. But there
are always new ways of squaring the circle just around the
next technological corner. At the centre of this group of
attitudes is late-Behaviourism with a touch of the Messianic
fixer, laced with an elaborate jargon compounded of some
applied social psychology plus some neurology plus some
technology. Pangloss is reborn in every generation.

Objectively, publicly, politically the realities are harsh; and
they are not to be wished away or even eroded by technological
advances in themselves. For example, on any considered view
of their possible contribution to developing understanding the
mass media are misused or misunderstood in most countries of
the world. By politicians, who once they are in power channel
the uses of the media to their own ends, or would if they could;
by intellectuals, who ignore them or make easy judgements on
them and so leave their fate to the politicians or to commercial
pressures. You look over a virtually world-wide panorama of
the media in chains: in chains to the foolish and narrowing
purposes of selling (always foolish and narrowing in their
effects on the medium); in chains to the narrowing and stifling
purposes of the national powers-that-be and their insistent,

fixed picture of what their culture is or ought to be. Here, an art really is 'made tongue-tied by authority'.

To a great many people modern societies seem deaf; it seems harder and harder to reach any 'genuine ... real ... authentic meeting ... confrontation ... dialogue ... encounter'. I am using those popular words—they have become clichés, in fact—deliberately, because their common qualities point quite plainly to what is felt to be missed: a sense of a meeting between human beings. Even those big exercises in communications designed to alert us all, as individuals, to some public danger, to 'increase our awareness' as they say, too often look like substitutes for responsible personal action. Small wonder some people settle for unilateral opting out. I think they are mistaken, but it is up to me to justify my position; in general the evidence runs their way.

Direct old-style rudeness is less off-putting than those computer-programmed relationships which make you into an object not a person, an object that has to be looked after maybe, but not known. Of course, we can't know all the people we are likely to meet in a lifetime nowadays; we need conventions for decent distancing. I do not object to those. I do object to carefully calculated closings of the distance for the sake of a temporary imitation of contact. Still, criticizing others isn't going to get us far. We have to start with ourselves, with our own difficulties in saying what we mean, with finding a language fluent enough to express our individuality, our vulnerability, and our wish for direct and honest contact.

We have to start at home, within our own society. If we can't get in touch there, there is not much hope further afield. But the balance between home and away is tricky. Over-immersion in one's own culture is far more common than internationalism without roots. Think of the many thousands of people who give so much attention to clubs or other organizations which are supposed to express some great national tradition, usually military or monarchist. Sunday mornings in uniform. You can meet them all over the world and, though their decorations differ, their expressions are alike. Can such national groups talk to each other? I doubt whether they could swop anything except bits of medal ribbon. If you are culture-bound to this degree you have become stiff-necked. Most cultures have a good or at least a favourite national drink, curious ways of greeting when they drink, peasants with pithy down-to-earth sayings, rich stores of wise saws and rugged metaphors, heroes of wars won and lost, strange rituals with flags and the like on set days, and other items in the galleries of national cultural bed-warmers. To think these are grounds on which we are likely to appreciate cultures other than our own is to guess that from the clash of cultural generalities or the swopping of odd paraphernalia precise comparative observations can come. To be caught up in that kind of thing hinders the appreciation of other cultures and of your own; and it keeps you out of touch with yourself.

There was an interesting contrast on the government committee on broadcasting on which I served. A Welsh witness harangued the committee on the dangers to Welsh culture: something had to be done at once, she said, or the culture would be irretrievably lost. That there was this acute danger was chiefly the fault of the English, and especially of the stuff they pumped into Wales through the mass media. The answer, we were told, was to let Wales have its own television channel just as it already had a radio channel for extensive broadcasting in Welsh. The English would have to find the money. It would be dear, but little enough repayment for all the ills the Welsh had suffered at the hands of the English. Then a truly Welsh culture could be put down that channel for several hours a day. The new technological world would come to the aid of the old.

As I said in an earlier lecture, the rights of minorities are not sufficiently recognized in broadcasting. This is especially true of television, partly because television costs so much to run, partly because minorities are generally squeezed out by the pressure to centralize networks. I quoted the incident above, not because I am against the principle of television provision for minorities—I am not—but because it was a classic cameo of cultural chauvinism; in this instance very aggressive chauvinism, combined with the wish to use the mass media for predetermined external ends. The strongest objection to such people is that, if they got what they wanted, the cultures they presided over would be unrepresentative of even their own people; they would be narrow and incapable of change. Later, in Scotland, a man from the Highlands told the same committee on broadcasting that there was a lot he regretted in the changes going on all around, but a lot he could not regret. He described how he tried to make the changes carry over with them some of the best in the old way of life, and he ended by saying: 'You can't put a ring fence round a culture'.

That is true. No culture has the whole truth or a truth so particular that it will be irreparably violated by contact with others. We can connect, we have to connect; not by hand-across-the-sea junketings nor by the solemnities of most attempts at international understanding but by a fully-faced realising of common qualities, the ribs of the universal human grammar. If we are going to respond anything like fully to cultures not our own it helps to have known, known sensitively and intelligently, our own culture. Our own culture will be a prison unless we can get above it and become in a certain sense cultureless, international. Yet internationalism is going to be a shallow grave unless we know something about what roots are, and how strongly they affect us all our lives.

When I started to prepare these lectures I knew roughly the area I was going to work in. I knew to some extent the kinds of things I wanted to say. I did not know how much I would find the argument altering as I went along, or what new things I would discover on the way. I didn't know, for instance, how often important elements in the argument were felt inside me as paradoxes; and I have still not quite worked out what that means. I knew I would criticize most established explanations of English life; I did not know how sharply I would criticize the explanations often accepted by intellectuals. I knew I wanted to say that the approach of many politicians to mass communications is bossy or *simpliste*; but I have said so more strongly than I expected. I did not realize how far I had gone away from overall, unitary, explanatory theories and programmes for sudden large-scale reform, how much I had come round to settling for gradual work, punching airholes till you can get your hand and arm and then your body through; gradual gains, not out of timidity but because the alternatives all look worse.

I had guessed the shock of trying to think about culture and communication from outside Britain, from this strange one-foot-in France-one-in-an-international-agency position, would be a big one. I did not realize till quite late in the preparation of these lectures how much two groups of assumptions lay under everything I said; or how much I would come to recognize that those assumptions, so much taken for granted at home, seem strange in large areas even of what is called the developed world.

I now realize much more sharply how I have simply taken for granted the primacy of the individual conscience, the belief that any wider commitment has to start from and satisfy that conviction. So the first group of assumptions can be got together around a statement like this: the individual matters, and he matters more than the society. It seems so simple to agree to this, but when you look around the world you see that few assume it or, if they professedly believe it, will honour it; and the deniers and ignorers are often in power. Moving out from that core statement, we come upon the related ideas: that the attempt at speaking honestly, first to yourself and to your nearest and dearest, matters and that it is the essential basis for speaking honestly on a wider front; that the commitment to truth matters and makes special pleading of all ideologies; that, though to reach the truth is difficult and we may never be finally objective, though our responses are always affected by culture and to some extent relativist, we are not in an absolute sense culture-bound. We can go a long way, by trying hard, towards stripping ourselves of hidden biases. The fact that no single one of us can be quite objective does not justify imposing a single ideological position on all the individuals in any one society. Individual opinions are not aberrations or self-indulgences; they are the only foundation for collective positions which do not deny the fullness of human nature. I know that there still exist societies where traditionally the collectivity has counted for more than the individual. I am not talking about such societies. I am talking about the insistence in some large modern societies on obedience to the state as an entity and to its ideology. An ideology is always less than a culture, and a state is always less than a community.

It follows that there is what feels like an absolute difference in kind, a difference a great many people are given little opportunity to recognize, between a disinterested statement or analysis or exploration, made by a man free to go to the limits of his own strengths, weaknesses and courage, and all those other kinds of trimming which so greatly outnumber disinterested work: from low-level prejudiced proselytizing to plainly doctored history, to middlebrow having-it-both-ways fashions, to bland high-level intellectual acrobatics within the ring of a pre-set philosophy—one into which the shock of any other way of seeing reality is not allowed to penetrate. Then you realize that for most people all over the world virtually everything that is publicly offered, in print or over the air, is *interested*, meant to tickle their fancies or arouse their emotions or hammer them for the sake of some other purpose—to get their money or their votes, to sell to them and go on selling, to keep them in line; not because the truth is great, and should prevail. If you have been much used to disinterested writing it is almost physically claustrophobic to read this stuff for any length of time. Reading the lower-level material is like passing your days in a waxworks show; all those set and painted imitations with no sense of depth, whether of character or of time. Reading the higher-level stuff you feel terribly sad at the extent to which intellectuals and artists can be redefined or will redefine themselves so as to fit a particular national position. At this point the sense of loss becomes so strong you are tempted to think the relativists are right, that all our talk of free men trying to describe themselves and their experiences as they find them, so as to increase their own insight and that of those who may care to listen, that all this is just an attractive delusion. If this is so, and since one would not want to be the other kind of writer or artist, a calculator or a servicer, the best course may be to have nothing to do with any profession in which we are expected to speak to each other outside our own circle; but to get a job working with neutral materials, cleaning streets or looking after forests, and confine our attempts to be in touch to our day-by-day, face-to-face, private and chosen and known circles. But that rather attractive despair would be premature. The roll-call of people who, even within systems which do not recognize their right to do so, have asserted through art and politics and religion the power, the independence and the courage that human beings are capable of is too long to justify backing out now.

This group of assumptions, I said earlier, contains the idea that men wish to reach what they insist on calling the truth, wish to write not for the sake of 'our society' or 'our people' but because it matters to tell things as they are, because it matters to—in a lovely phrase—'give things their proper names'; that men wish to reach others on that basis, not as a large block but as individuals each of whom also respects the search for truth; that larger groupings are justified by the assent all the individuals within them have given to a value *outside* them or the larger group—the respect for truth; that when a man says: 'Whatsoever is beautiful, whatsoever is of good report ...' he is talking about something he believes he can from time to time recognize and hopes he would continue to recognize even under pressure to deny it, something that is worth his love and loyalty, something bound up with his self-respect. He may feel unable to say unequivocally; 'The truth is great and shall prevail'; but even if he were publicly to deny the truth under stress he hopes that in his heart of hearts he would still know that he *had* denied the truth.

So these assumptions contain also the idea that a man ought to be free to try to live up to those ideals, as a matter of his own choice, not hindered, even if not helped, by the powers outside; that he is free, it follows, to criticize the status quo if his sense of the truth leads him that way; that he has some room for action as an individual and as a member of groups other than those arranged by, or smiled upon by, the authorities, room for action which seems to him right.

From there it is only a short step to the idea that a healthy society ought to have within it many voices arguing in different ways, including especially voices arguing against the prevailing outlook; that a society ought to be able to stand such a strain direct rather than to prohibit or employ elaborate cancelling-out and corralling devices so as to drain criticism and counter-arguments of any force. Societies, like people, have a natural skill at reducing irritants; they have complicated ways, not all of them deliberately decided on by the authorities, of trying to ensure that free speech is made futile; and sometimes it seems as though they have succeeded. But that is not so. In some places now and again, perhaps in most places from time to time, something gets through: the law defies the government to give what seems the just judgement; the broadcasters defy the authorities and say exactly what did happen; and the Press, against its own commercial interests, does the same; some teachers refuse to put out a line they know to be biased. Keeping up that pressure on all fronts is one of the best and hardest things we can do.

I am still teasing at the ramifications of those first assumptions and I reach down now to an even more basic sense, one which underpins the wish itself to speak straight to one another. It is the idea, which I used never to think about, but I now find it extraordinary, strange and compelling, of fellow-feeling; fellow-feeling based not on the fact that we all belong to a particular national culture, are Frenchmen or Russians or Americans or British, nor on an abstract internationalist commitment, but based on recognizing our common experience, and on realizing that it is the facing of common sorrows which above all links us. Then I always remember Keats' quietly astonishing remark; 'Men, I think, should bear with one another'; or Yeats' old men looking out at the world: 'Gaiety transfiguring all that dread'; or a less well-known statement but of the same general kind, George Orwell's about the postcards of Donald McGill—the cards you can buy at the seaside, full of middle-aged wives with enormous bums, and little beery husbands leering at what used to be called 'flappers', and nagging mothers-in-law. After he had looked at the cards for a long time, Orwell said: 'When it comes to the pinch, human beings are heroic'. One will go a long way with a man who can look at what seems shabby and unheroic material and come up with a conclusion like that. Against such phrases I always find myself setting another, one which chills the blood. Far from seeing men as brothers, it sees them as things to be manipulated; a cold, baleful eye looks through you, calculating the odds, and someone says:

Stone dead hath no fellow.

The sense of fellow-feeling denies all abstractings, all hierarchies and all rationalizations; it provides the basis—the only basis— for moving out beyond national cultures to make contact wherever someone else is willing and free to listen.

I remember, on first reading Dostoevsky, being impressed by a scene in which a father is humiliated before his small son. He is humiliated to the depths of his spirit at being so lowered in the eyes of one for whom he had been, naturally, up to that moment a great man. It is not a matter of the father's pride in himself, but of his love and concern for the boy. For me that scene marks one of those moments when the sense of common feeling bridges centuries and hundreds of miles and great differences between societies, a moment when one has a sudden and intense flood of sympathy because someone has looked directly and fully at his experience, and shared it. I am not putting up a theory of intense moments in literature; I am using such a moment as a way of pointing to one of the essential elements in full communication, the recognition of fellow-feeling.

Of my two main assumptions, the second is that we can in fact reach each other. These talks have simply assumed we can; they have started from that point as though it were an undeniable truth. It is not; it is a very large and, so far as I know, unproven assertion. It is possible, and to some people seems inescapable, to decide that in the end we do not communicate, and indeed do not really care or seek to communicate; that what we call our wish to communicate is only a saving, a face-saving, way of describing the wish to hear ourselves speak, to make others into mirrors of ourselves, to make them temporarily enter our private universes, so that we shall not feel so lonely, so that those private universes shall seem more valid. So that when we claim to have been in touch with someone else we are only really saying that the echo-chamber has worked, that we have heard come back to ourselves the gratifying echoes of our own voices. The circle is complete, closed, vicious, not to be escaped from.

I have argued that communication starts with trying to speak more honestly to yourself, that it can then if we wish move out to trying to speak to others, and that it sometimes succeeds. But all those are acts of faith. I find such phrases as: 'Now and forever we are not alone' and 'We are members one of another' moving. Perhaps that is because of the beauty of the language. But I want to call them right and true too, in their suggestion that our attempts to come together are not simply defensive groupings by existential galley-slaves, or huddlings together by frightened kittens, but something more: a sign that we have a regard for the truth and a wish truthfully to discuss the nature of our common lives. So we are seeking a kind of comfort, yes, but not only a cowardly or self-flattering comfort. I believe all that, even though I cannot prove it.

Which means, I also believe, that when we listen we do sometimes try to listen fully, are not all the time as we listen operating that elaborate selecting-machine which picks out for reception only those elements in what is being said that we are willing to take at any moment, those which suit our psychic books in one way or another, which flatter us or amuse us or at least do not disturb us. That process does go on, much of the time. But not always, not all the time.

But of all this too there is no proof, no proof that either side finally communicates anything accurately. Our whole world of discourse, when you begin to look at it, proves to be full of incredibly large assumptions of this kind. We are like the insects called pond-skaters: we assume that there is a skin over the water of our shared experience and then set out across it and hope to meet, because if we assumed otherwise we would sink without trace.

What I have been calling my two main groups of assumptions, that it matters to communicate and that one can communicate, are inseparable; or, better, they have a common source. They come together in yet another unprovable assumption: that experience is exchangeable; in what I called representativeness in the second of these talks; in the assumption that our personal experiences can have a more than personal meaning, can be shared, can be typical, symbolic, significant.

My two main assumptions are joined in yet another way. If we felt at bottom that we were always doctoring our experiences, our attempts to reach others would all be forms of salesmanship, not attempts to tell things as they are.

The urge to communicate and the idea that experience is shared both rest on the belief that we can, at least sometimes, look at our experiences straight; and on the belief that it is important to tell people about them because other people count as we feel we count ourselves; in other words, this kind of effort at communication rests on a feeling—I called it a fellow-feeling—towards others which is intrinsically different from one which wishes only to use them or manipulate them, or from an ancient mariner's grabbing them by the lapel so as to get something off his chest.

I think, then, that an adequate approach to communication has to be founded on these main beliefs. I have said they are unprovable; but we all believe more than we can prove: that the truth to experience against all preconceptions matters; that men matter to each other; that our experience pushes us out to find a common ground of feeling and of judgement; that our wish to tell and to listen is more than disguised self-seeking or self-involvement, and that that shared wish is sometimes gratified.